TECUMSEH

TECUMSEH
Shawnee Rebel

Robert Cwiklik

Senior Consulting Editor
W. David Baird
Howard A. White Professor of History
Pepperdine University

CHELSEA HOUSE PUBLISHERS

New York   Philadelphia

FRONTISPIECE Tecumseh appears in non-Indian attire in this 1810 portrait. After he created the Indian solidarity movement, the warrior-diplomat usually wore the Shawnees' traditional garb, a simple leather breechcloth and scalp lock.

ON THE COVER This image of Tecumseh began as a pencil sketch drawn about 1808 by Pierre Le Dru, a French trader in Vincennes, Indiana Territory. Some 50 years later, an unidentified artist added a cap, medal, and the costume of a British brigadier general, Tecumseh's rank during the War of 1812.

Chelsea House Publishers
EDITOR-IN-CHIEF Richard S. Papale
EXECUTIVE MANAGING EDITOR Karyn Gullen Browne
COPY CHIEF Philip Koslow
PICTURE EDITOR Adrian G. Allen
ART DIRECTOR Nora Wertz
MANUFACTURING DIRECTOR Gerald Levine
SYSTEMS MANAGER Lindsey Ottman
PRODUCTION COORDINATOR Marie Claire Cebrián-Ume

North American Indians of Achievement
SENIOR EDITOR Liz Sonneborn

Staff for TECUMSEH
TEXT EDITOR Marian W. Taylor
COPY EDITOR Danielle Janusz
EDITORIAL ASSISTANT Nicole Greenblatt
DESIGNER Debora Smith
PICTURE RESEARCHER Lisa Kirchner
COVER ILLUSTRATION Shelley Pritchett

Printed and bound in Mexico.

3 5 7 9 8 6 4

Library of Congress Cataloging-in-Publication Data

Cwiklik, Robert.
Tecumseh, Shawnee Rebel/Robert Cwiklik
  p. cm.—(North American Indians of achievement)
Includes bibliographical references and index.
Summary: A biography of the Shawnee warrior, orator, and leader who united a confederacy of Indians in an effort to save Indian land from the advance of white soldiers and settlers.
ISBN 0-7910-1721-4
ISBN 0-7910-1956-X (pbk.)
1. Tecumseh, Shawnee Chief, 1768–1813—Juvenile literature. 2. Shawnee Indians—Biography—Juvenile literature. 3. Shawnee Indians—History—Juvenile literature. [1. Tecumseh, Shawnee Chief, 1768–1813. 2. Shawnee Indians—Biography. 3. Indians of North America—Biography.] I. Title. II. Series.
E99.S35T1174 1993   92-21656
973'.0497302—dc20   CIP
[B] [92]   AC

CONTENTS

NORTH AMERICAN INDIANS OF ACHIEVEMENT

Other titles in preparation

ON INDIAN LEADERSHIP

by W. David Baird
Howard A. White Professor of History
Pepperdine University

Authoritative utterance is in thy mouth, perception is in thy heart, and thy tongue is the shrine of justice," the ancient Egyptians said of their king. From him, the Egyptians expected authority, discretion, and just behavior. Homer's *Iliad* suggests that the Greeks demanded somewhat different qualities from their leaders: justice and judgment, wisdom and counsel, shrewdness and cunning, valor and action. It is not surprising that different people living at different times should seek different qualities from the individuals they looked to for guidance. By and large, a people's requirements for leadership are determined by two factors: their culture and the unique circumstances of the time and place in which they live.

Before the late 15th century, when non-Indians first journeyed to what is now North America, most Indian tribes were not ruled by a single person. Instead, there were village chiefs, clan headmen, peace chiefs, war chiefs, and a host of other types of leaders, each with his or her own specific duties. These influential people not only decided political matters but also helped shape their tribe's social, cultural, and religious life. Usually, Indian leaders held their positions because they had won the respect of their peers. Indeed, if a leader's followers at any time decided that he or she was out of step with the will of the people, they felt free to look to someone else for advice and direction.

Thus, the greatest achievers in traditional Indian communities were men and women of extraordinary talent. They were not only skilled at navigating the deadly waters of tribal politics and cultural customs but also able to, directly or indirectly, make a positive and significant difference in the daily life of their followers.

From the beginning of their interaction with Native Americans, non-Indians failed to understand these features of Indian leadership. Early European explorers and settlers merely assumed that Indians had the same relationship with their leaders as non-Indians had with their kings and queens. European monarchs generally inherited their positions and ruled large nations however they chose, often with little regard for the desires or needs of their subjects. As a result, the settlers of Jamestown saw Pocahontas as a "princess" and Pilgrims dubbed Wampanoag leader Metacom "King Philip," envisioning them in roles very different from those in which their own people placed them.

As more and more non-Indians flocked to North America, the nature of Indian leadership gradually began to change. Influential Indians no longer had to take on the often considerable burden of pleasing only their own people; they also had to develop a strategy of dealing with the non-Indian newcomers. In a rapidly changing world, new types of Indian role models with new ideas and talents continually emerged. Some were warriors; others were peacemakers. Some held political positions within their tribes; others were writers, artists, religious prophets, or athletes. Although the demands of Indian leadership altered from generation to generation, several factors that determined which Indian people became prominent in the centuries after first contact remained the same.

Certain personal characteristics distinguished these Indians of achievement. They were intelligent, imaginative, practical, daring, shrewd, uncompromising, ruthless, and logical. They were constant in friendships, unrelenting in hatreds, affectionate with their relatives, and respectful to their God or gods. Of course, no single Native American leader embodied all these qualities, nor these qualities only. But it was these characteristics that allowed them to succeed.

The special skills and talents that certain Indians possessed also brought them to positions of importance. The life of Hiawatha, the legendary founder of the powerful Iroquois Confederacy, displays the value that oratorical ability had for many Indians in power.

The biography of Cochise, the 19th-century Apache chief, illustrates that leadership often required keen diplomatic skills not only in transactions among tribespeople but also in hardheaded negotiations with non-Indians. For others, such as Mohawk Joseph Brant and Navajo Peter MacDonald, a non-Indian education proved advantageous in their dealings with other peoples.

Sudden changes in circumstance were another crucial factor in determining who became influential in Indian communities. King Philip in the 1670s and Geronimo in the 1880s both came to power when their people were searching for someone to lead them into battle against white frontiersmen who had forced upon them a long series of indignities. Seeing the rising discontent of Indians of many tribes in the 1810s, Tecumseh and his brother, the Shawnee prophet Tenskwatawa, proclaimed a message of cultural revitalization that appealed to thousands. Other Indian achievers recognized cooperation with non-Indians as the most advantageous path during their lifetime. Sarah Winnemucca in the late 19th century bridged the gap of understanding between her people and their non-Indian neighbors through the publication of her autobiography *Life Among the Piutes*. Olympian Jim Thorpe in the early 20th century championed the assimilationist policies of the U.S. government and, with his own successes, demonstrated the accomplishments Indians could make in the non-Indian world. And Wilma Mankiller, principal chief of the Cherokees, continues to fight successfully for the rights of her people through the courts and through negotiation with federal officials.

Leadership among Native Americans, just as among all other peoples, can be understood only in the context of culture and history. But the centuries that Indians have had to cope with invasions of foreigners in their homelands have brought unique hardships and obstacles to the Native American individuals who most influenced and inspired others. Despite these challenges, there has never been a lack of Indian men and women equal to these tasks. With such strong leaders, it is no wonder that Native Americans remain such a vital part of this nation's cultural landscape.

1

THE HEAD OF THEM ALL

Indiana Territory governor William Henry Harrison scanned the road for his guests, a delegation of Shawnees led by the warrior Tecumseh. Harrison planned to receive the Indians on the veranda of his mansion, where a breeze from the Wabash River might offer some relief from the blistering midwestern summer. This day, a Monday in August 1810, had dawned hot, and it promised to get hotter.

Harrison was an old hand at dealing with Indians. Representing the United States, he had persuaded many Indian leaders to give up huge tracts of tribal land without a fight. By 1810, the 37-year-old Virginian had gained a secure reputation as both military leader and civil administrator. To many, he personified the qualities most admired on the frontier: ability, courage, decisiveness.

As governor of the vast Indiana Territory—a position he had held for 10 years—Harrison reigned supreme. Only the president of the United States could give him orders, and the president rarely did. Harrison held the power of life and death over all the souls in his domain; he could, in short, write his own law. If ever a man radiated strength and self-confidence, it was William Henry Harrison. But as he paced the veranda on this August morning, Harrison looked nervous.

Tecumseh, 42 years old when he met Governor William Henry Harrison in Vincennes, Indiana, in 1810, made a powerful impression on observers. A U.S. Army captain called the six-foot-tall Shawnee chief "one of the finest looking men I ever saw . . . a daring, bold looking fellow."

11

Tecumseh, who had arrived in Vincennes a few days earlier, had, in fact, put the whole town's nerves on edge. Looking like anything but a friendly visiting leader, he had shown up with an awesome flotilla of 80 war canoes and more than 400 armed warriors. His men, noted one army captain, "were all painted in the most terrific manner," their canoes "well prepared for war." Tecumseh himself was impressive, standing tall and straight in the lead canoe, powerful muscles rippling on his bare arms and back. He was "one of the finest looking men I ever saw," observed the captain, "about six feet high, straight, with large, fine features, and altogether a daring, bold looking fellow."

To Harrison's undoubted relief, Tecumseh seemed peaceful when he arrived at the mansion on Monday morning. As he had promised, the Shawnee leader left most of his entourage camped outside town. Accompanying him was only a small band of bodyguards who, like their leader, wore buckskin breechclouts and leggings rather than war dress.

Settlers and Indians engage in a day of brisk trading in an Indiana Territory village. By 1810, the year Tecumseh confronted Harrison about the illegal acquisition of Indian lands, outposts like this one studded the frontier.

Harrison, a tall man with a long nose, a craggy chin, and smoldering, deep-set eyes, rose at Tecumseh's approach. Behind the governor stood his own entourage: several army officers in full dress uniform, a group of local politicians in formal suits, a sprinkling of "friendly" Indian chiefs in colorful headdresses, and about a dozen soldiers in battle gear.

Harrison expected to hold the meeting in his mansion, but 100 yards from the porch, Tecumseh brought his group to a sudden halt. The Shawnee war chief, reported an interpreter, wanted to meet not in the governor's home but in a grove of trees nearby. Obligingly, Harrison strode out and told Tecumseh that the Great White Father in Washington had asked him to show the Indians every courtesy. He would have chairs brought outside.

Tecumseh was silent for a moment. Then he looked upward. "My father?" he said. "The Great Spirit is my father, the earth is my mother, and on her bosom I will recline." With that, he and his warriors settled themselves on the grass. The formally dressed men of the governor's party raised their eyebrows and exchanged glances, then perched on the wooden chairs carried out by the soldiers. It would not be the last time Tecumseh would unsettle the white men this day.

Seeds for the 1810 Vincennes meeting had been planted a year earlier. It began with Harrison's ambitious dream of making his Indiana Territory a full-fledged state. Before it could attain statehood, the territory would have to meet federal population requirements by luring another 60,000 settlers, all of whom would need plots on which to build their homesteads. Much of the territory was still claimed by Indians, but Harrison proposed to straighten that out with a new round of negotiations.

In dealing with Native Americans, Harrison was accustomed to having his way. In 1809, for example, he had successfully negotiated a treaty between the United

States and the Indians of the Old Northwest (the immense area between the Great Lakes and the Ohio and Mississippi rivers). After sending secret bribes to a group of "friendly" Indian leaders, he had invited them to a council in Fort Wayne.

There, surrounded by hundreds of well-armed soldiers, Harrison told the chiefs that the United States wished to buy their land. His government, he pointed out, could simply seize the acreage by force, but it was prepared to make a generous payment instead. He advised the Indians to sell the land while the Americans were still in the mood to buy it.

Some of the Indians were loath to accept Harrison's plan, but others, notably the Potawatomi chief Winnemac, argued the dissenters down. In the end, the Indians signed the Fort Wayne Treaty on Harrison's terms: for $7,000 worth of goods and the promise of an additional $1,750 worth each year thereafter, they parted with three million acres.

Such questionable land deals were common in the first decade of the 19th century. Many Americans believed that Indians had no real title to the land, no need for so much of it, and no will to resist further encroachment. Driven from their villages by the endless onslaught of settlers, often living in squalid refugee camps outside U.S. Army forts, and surviving on government handouts, Native Americans seemed a beaten people.

Indians angered by the land sales sometimes raided American settlements; in revenge, settlers attacked and burned Indian villages. Blood flowed freely on both sides, with the Indians most often the losers. Usually isolated and heavily outnumbered and outgunned, they were no match for the whites and their awesome firepower.

Still, Americans worried that Indians would one day organize a united resistance, perhaps aided by British troops from Canada. British-American relations had been

tense ever since the American victory in the Revolutionary War, and Harrison and others feared that the British
would ally themselves with the Indians in a new war
against the United States. Equipped with British weapons
and supplies, a unified Indian army would be a very
serious threat.

Before Harrison negotiated the Fort Wayne Treaty, he
had learned about a rapidly expanding multitribal movement aimed at resisting—with violence if necessary—
further land sales to the Americans. Leading the
movement was Tenskwatawa, a Shawnee holy man also
known as the Prophet. The Fort Wayne Treaty stoked
the fires of Indian resistance, and bands of angry warriors
had begun to surge into Prophetstown, Tenskwatawa's
Wabash River headquarters north of Vincennes.

Planning to intimidate the Shawnee holy man, Harrison invited him to travel to Washington, D.C., to meet
the Great White Father, President James Madison. The
trappings of wealth and power in the nation's capital,
thought the governor, would overawe Tenskwatawa (as
it had other chiefs) and make him see that Indians could
never defeat so mighty a nation.

But Tenskwatawa refused to visit Washington. Fur-
thermore, he declined to go to Vincennes to meet with
Harrison. In response to the governor's request for his
appearance, Tenskwatawa sent word that his brother
Tecumseh would come instead. Harrison had never
believed Tenskwatawa capable of leading a serious uprising against the United States, but he had reason for
concern about the Prophet's brother. The governor had
recently received reports suggesting that Tecumseh—
known as "the Moses of the family"—might be the real
force behind the resistance.

Now, seated in a grove of trees along the Wabash,
Tecumseh faced Harrison across the grass. There was
something about this strong-featured, self-assured war

chief that commanded respect, even from the governor. Tecumseh broke the silence first, his voice calm and measured but his words cold and sharp. He began by reviewing the history of white-Indian relations in North America, an account crowded with injustices suffered by Indians at the hands of whites. He talked for a long time, citing treaty after treaty made by the whites, each containing promises that the whites would ask for no more Indian land, each broken in turn. Much of the Indians' former domain, he pointed out, was now thickly settled with whites.

Tecumseh next turned to the subject of the day's meeting. Despite the abuses Indians had suffered in the past, he noted, some years ago they had agreed to abide by yet another agreement—the Treaty of Greenville—which drew still another boundary between the lands of Indians and those of others. The non-Indians had promised, as always, that they would never cross this new line. But settlers did so routinely, taking what they wanted by force.

Now, not 20 years later, Tecumseh continued, Harrison had broken his people's word again, proposing the Fort Wayne Treaty and demanding still more Indian territory. Indians were constantly being driven farther and farther west. "The Great Spirit gave this great island to his red children," Tecumseh told Harrison. "He placed the whites on the other side of the big water. They were not contented with their own, but came to take ours from us. They have driven us from the sea to the lakes—we can go no farther."

Tecumseh accused Harrison and his allies of turning Indians against one another to gain their objectives. The chiefs whom the governor had invited to Fort Wayne were said to be the "owners" of Indian land, with the authority to sell it. But no one, asserted Tecumseh, had

Tecumseh's younger brother Tenskwatawa led a life of drunken idleness until 1805, when he went into a coma, recovered, and proclaimed himself the Great Spirit's messenger. He pleased whites by preaching honesty and sobriety, but he frightened and infuriated them by denouncing Indian land sales.

the authority to sell that land. It was the common property of all Indians, not of any one tribe.

This statement, said Tecumseh, was not based simply on his own wishes. He had met with all the tribes of the Northwest, and all had agreed to stop acting as separate groups, and to act instead as one people to defend—with their lives, if necessary—their remaining land. Tecumseh asserted that he had been authorized to speak for the newly united Indians: "I am the head of them all," he said.

He and his people, Tecumseh warned, would never accept the Fort Wayne Treaty, which had been approved only by greedy and cowardly village chiefs. There would be no peace, he said, unless Harrison canceled the treaty. "If you do not," Tecumseh told Harrison, "it will appear as if you wished me to kill all the chiefs that sold you this land."

Then Harrison took his turn, contradicting Tecumseh with every word he spoke: Indians were not one people; if their god had wanted them united, he would have given them the same language. Indians were an assortment of different tribes, each self-governing, each speaking its own tongue, each owning certain lands. The chiefs who sold land to the United States had every legal and moral right to do so.

Now Tecumseh's gaze focused on Winnemac, one of the "friendly" chiefs who had cooperated in the last land sale. Then, in an uncharacteristic burst of rage, he began to shout in the Shawnee language, calling Winnemac a traitor who had tricked senile old men into signing the Fort Wayne Treaty. At this, Winnemac drew a pistol from his cloak and began to load it. Instantly, Tecumseh's men encircled him, their war clubs and tomahawks raised. At the same time, the soldiers rushed forward and aimed their muskets, and the civilians seized pieces of firewood.

Harrison drew his sword. For a moment, Harrison and Tecumseh glared at one another soundlessly.

Then Harrison ordered his men to lower their weapons and asked Winnemac what Tecumseh had just said. Wanting to cast the Shawnee in the worst possible light, Winnemac testified falsely. Tecumseh, he said, had accused the governor personally of cheating the Indians; he had, in fact, openly called him a liar.

Facing the Shawnee warrior with an icy stare, Harrison said he would not continue the talks. Because the Shawnees had come to the meeting under his protection, he added coldly, they were free to leave peacefully. Then he turned on his heel and, followed by his entourage, left the grove.

Tempers cooled off and the meetings went on for two more days, but they led nowhere. Possessed by incompatible dreams, Tecumseh and Harrison were separated by a chasm wide and deep. Tecumseh dreamed of preserving his people's traditional ways, of saving the

In a moment of hair-trigger tension, Tecumseh and Harrison face off in 1810. The confrontation between the Old Northwest's great adversaries would end in a draw — this time.

magnificent Old Northwest forests, of creating a multi-tribal, all-Indian nation. For his part, Harrison dreamed of a United States that would one day stretch from the Atlantic Ocean to the Pacific, and envisioned himself removing all obstacles in its path. In the landscape of that dream, Indians were just another obstacle.

As separate tribes, Indians presented only a small obstruction to Harrison's dream, but as a united Indian nation, they would pose a serious threat. Harrison accordingly tried hard to convince Indian leaders that the Americans would be offended by a unified front; the Indians were better off doing business tribe by tribe anyway, he said. Responding to that argument, Tecumseh said the tribes were following the example of the United States itself, which had formed a union among "all the fires" (the Indian term for states). The Indians had found no fault with that association, Tecumseh pointed out dryly. Why, then, should the whites object to an Indian union?

Tecumseh's knowledge and his skill at using it in argument continued to astonish Harrison. He realized this was a man to be reckoned with, a man Indians of all tribes might follow to their deaths. But despite his deep respect for Tecumseh, Harrison saw him and his movement as an acute and growing danger to the United States.

In the summer of 1811, the governor wrote to the secretary of war in Washington, asking for military reinforcements. His request, approved by President Madison himself, brought better results than Harrison had dared hope for. Into Vincennes rode the entire Fourth United States Regiment, a crack outfit made even stronger by the brigade of Kentucky sharpshooters who had joined it on the way. The Fourth U.S., along with the troops already stationed in the territory, would have one mission: to crush the Shawnee brothers.

2

THE PANTHER

Tecumseh was born in 1768 near Chalahgawtha, a Shawnee village at the site of what is now Oldtown, Ohio. His tribe, whose members lived mainly in communities between the Scioto and Miami rivers, was known far and wide for its shrewdness and independence. The Shawnees were also famed for their great skill and valor in combat; no one, Indian or white, wanted them as enemies.

Like most Native Americans, the Shawnees created myths to explain the world around them. One such story concerned a giant meteor, a dazzling shooting star that was really the Panther, one of the spirit world's mightiest beings. Although he was rarely seen by mortals, the Panther was said to pass across the sky each night, searching for a place to sleep. By day, he roamed the forest, springing on the wicked and aiding the good.

According to Shawnee records, the panther crossed the sky on March 9, 1768—at the exact moment that a male child was born to a Shawnee war chief and his wife. The boy's *unsoma*, or personal symbol, and his name were therefore ordained: Tecumseh, "the Panther Passing Across." It was an appropriate choice; in later years, Tecumseh's enemies would mark the resemblance between the powerful beast of legend and the powerful warrior of reality.

An Indian woman gathers fuel, suspending her burdens from a strap around her head. Although Tecumseh's mother, Methotasa, was the wife of an important Shawnee war chief, she performed the same daily chores as the other women of the tribe: tending children, cooking, collecting firewood, and raising crops.

21

The Shawnees consisted of five *septs*, or clans, each of which performed a special function for the tribe as a whole. Tecumseh was born into the Kispokotha sept, the group responsible for conducting wars. His father, Pucksinwah, was a revered war chief and diplomat. His mother, Methotasa, was a member of the Cherokee tribe. Kidnapped as a teenager by a Shawnee war party, she fell in love with and married the considerably older Pucksinwah soon after her capture. Pucksinwah and Methotasa were already the parents of a son, 12-year-old Chiksika, and a daughter, 10-year-old Tecumapese, when Tecumseh was born. Two years after Tecumseh's arrival, Methotasa amazed her husband and the rest of the community by giving birth to triplets—three more future Shawnee warriors.

Childbirth did not long interrupt the hard daily routine of a Shawnee woman. After bearing a child, she would quickly return to her many chores, which included tending fields of corn, peas, squash, and other crops. Little is known of Tecumseh's early life, but he was probably raised in the traditional manner of his people. As Methotasa worked, she must have kept an eye on her infant as most Indian women did, strapping him to a cradleboard that she either wore or hung from a nearby branch.

The Shawnees considered child rearing a communal responsibility: not only their parents, but all the tribe's adults watched over the youngsters. Shawnee toddlers were allowed to roam rather freely about the village. As soon as they were old enough, adults taught them to recognize their names as whistled, one note per syllable. When the boys grew up and became hunters and warriors, they used these whistling codes, along with imitations of bird songs and other animal cries, to communicate with one another in the forest.

Sketched by a frontier artist in 1796, a settler pauses in the doorway of her log-cabin home. A residence like this one could be built by a single frontiersman in two weeks— provided he was expert with an ax and willing to work about 18 hours a day.

While Shawnee women tended the fields, the men hunted for game, which supplied the tribe with both food and clothing. The tribe held a strong position in the Old Northwest. To the south, they controlled vast hunting grounds stretching deep into modern Kentucky and West Virginia; to the west, their territory ran far into what is now Indiana. But the Shawnees also faced a grave challenge: non-Indians were moving west, steadily encroaching on Indian land. As time passed, more and more Indians of the Old Northwest came to believe that a bloody showdown over the land question was inevitable.

The newcomers crippled the Indians' economy and upset their lifestyle in countless ways. One was the booming fur trade. Europeans, their own forests over-hunted, presented a rich market for North American furs. To obtain them, traders offered Indians a tempting assortment of manufactured goods: muskets, mirrors, steel hunting knives, iron skillets, and more. Eager to own such useful and curious items, Indians began overhunting their own forests, seriously depleting the animal population on which their economy depended.

Settlers further thinned the region's once-abundant game; as they steadily cleared forests and fenced pastures, wild animals fled. The newcomers even hunted for sport, a practice that Indians viewed as wasteful and unholy. For their part, settlers considered Indians wasteful. Non-Indian farmers and ranchers produced large harvests on relatively small plots of land; they could not understand why so few "savages" needed so many acres of virgin forest to supply their needs.

There had been a time—some two centuries before Tecumseh's birth—when native tribes reigned over the

"Generous" white traders offer whiskey to their Indian hosts. Under the influence of alcohol, which they had never encountered before, Native Americans often agreed to out-rageously unfair trade deals and land purchases.

In this mid-19th-century painting, artist Alfred Jacob Miller shows hunters circling a buffalo. Before 1850, some 100 million buffalo—essential to the Indians for food, clothing, and shelter—ranged the western plains, but by 1889, gun-happy settlers had reduced the animals' population to about 1,000.

whole of North America. That had begun to change in the early 16th century, when the Long Knives—the Indians' name for Europeans—started to pour into the New World, displace its original inhabitants, and put their own stamp on its culture.

By the mid-17th century, the non-Indian presence in North America had become an established fact of life for most Native Americans. And by the time of Tecumseh's birth, settlers had long since taken over the lands along the Atlantic coast; once inhabited by Indians, these lands were now 13 British colonies, largely populated by free white Europeans and enslaved black Africans.

Indians had also grown accustomed to seeing their forests become battlefields for European feuds—wars that had, in many cases, drawn in the Indians themselves. In the French and Indian War (1754–63), which finally settled the French-British struggle for control of North America, the Shawnees fought on the losing French side.

After the French defeat, the British hoped to take over the lucrative fur trade. Making a truce with the Shaw-

nees, the English promised to supply them with the European manufactured goods they had come to depend on. The mood of friendly cooperation, however, was short-lived. The French had treated the Indians as equal trading partners, but the British seemed to see themselves as superior beings, and they regularly cheated the Indians. The Indians deeply resented the Britons' high-handed attitude, but they were even more distressed by the steady flow of English settlers into their lands.

Aiming to thwart British expansion, Pontiac, a war chief of the Ottawa Indians, led the Shawnees and several other tribes in a 1763 revolt known as Pontiac's War. Most of the coalition's tribes—Shawnees, Delawares, Chippewas, Miamis, Potawatomies, Senecas, and Kick-apoos—had fought on the French side in the French and Indian War, and they expected the French to help them fight this campaign.

The French—who had encouraged Pontiac to revolt in the first place—declined to help their former allies, but Pontiac and his forces nevertheless ran up a string of remarkable victories, capturing or destroying 8 of the 10 British forts in the Great Lakes area. Alarmed by the

Returning to his camp near the Scioto River on May 1, 1774, Chief Logan of the Mingo tribe discovers the bodies of his family—one of them his pregnant sister— scalped and mutilated by a gang of white fur traders. The murders horrified Americans of all races.

Indians' military successes, the British turned to the 18th-century equivalent of germ warfare. In the summer of 1763, they began to send the tribes gifts: blankets infected with smallpox. Utterly vulnerable to the contagious disease, thousands of Indians died, crippling Pontiac's legions and forcing him to sign a peace treaty in 1764.

Meanwhile, fearing that chaos on the frontier would weaken its authority, the British government took steps to keep the Indians peaceful. The first move was clarifying the boundary between British and Indian territory. Soon after Pontiac began his revolt, King George III of England issued the Proclamation of 1763, an emergency order that forbade westbound settlers, fur traders, or speculators to cross a line drawn along the top of the Allegheny Mountains.

A proclamation issued thousands of miles away, however, had little effect on eager American settlers, who scoffed at the 1763 line and continued to pour into Indian lands. Predictably, the Indians retaliated by killing the intruders. Opposition to the Proclamation of 1763 grew so strong that the British revised their western policy; in 1765, they began signing new Indian treaties. In 1768, the year of Tecumseh's birth, the British signed the Treaty of Fort Stanwix (New York) with the Iroquois Indians of the Northeast. Under the treaty, the Iroquois ceded to the British a large spread of land west of the Appalachians, including Indiana.

There was only one problem: the territory did not belong to the Iroquois. Most of it, in fact, consisted of traditional Shawnee hunting grounds. Such fine points, however, meant little to whites. When word spread that Kentucky was "an earthly paradise," settlers poured in.

In the spring of 1774, tensions between Indians and settlers exploded when a group of frontiersmen massacred 13 Indian women and children on the Scioto River. The murders outraged Indians and colonists alike: future United States president Thomas Jefferson, for example, called the killings "inhuman and indecent." The incident not only shocked the settlers but also terrified them. Whites now feared that the Indians would seek revenge with a bloody, full-scale uprising.

Determined to stop such violence before it started, the governor of Virginia, Lord Dunmore, made a preemptive move: he raised a militia of 1,500 volunteers and set out to destroy the Shawnee towns on the Scioto River. Shawnee scouts had tracked the militia's movements, and the tribe was prepared to meet the attackers with a force of 700 warriors. Most of these fighters were Shawnees, but they also included Mingos, Wyandots, and Delawares who did not agree with their passive chiefs. Commanding the warriors was the Shawnee war chief Cornstalk, whose lieutenants included Tecumseh's father, Pucksinwah. The conflict between the two forces would become known as Lord Dunmore's War.

Early in the morning of October 10, 1774, the warriors ambushed the Virginia militiamen at Point Pleasant, an ironically named hilltop at the junction of the Great Kanawha and Ohio rivers. The day's casualties would include some 100 militiamen and about 50 warriors—one of them Pucksinwah. After some six hours of intense battle, a rifle ball had slammed into his chest, mortally wounding him but leaving him a few moments to speak.

Pucksinwah addressed his dying words to his eldest son, Chiksika, who had been fighting alongside his father. The war chief asked his 14-year-old son to swear he would never make peace with the settlers and that he would care for his family and see to his younger brothers' training as warriors. Chiksika carried his father's body across the river, then tied it upright on the saddle of his horse. Mounted behind the dead man, the grieving boy rode back to his family.

Scottish-born John Murray, fourth earl of Dunmore, served as royal governor of Virginia from 1771 to 1776. Afraid that the massacre of Chief Logan's family would provoke an Indian reprisal, he undertook Lord Dunmore's War, a conflict that ended in the Battle of Point Pleasant and the death of Pucksinwah, Tecumseh's father.

Cornstalk led his surviving men up the Scioto River to Chillicothe, where he convened a war council. The situation was grim: the militia was advancing on the Shawnee villages from two directions. Most Shawnee men were out on the warpath, leaving the villages' women, children, and old people defenseless. Cornstalk feared that if the warriors pursued the nearby militiamen, other soldiers would descend on the Shawnee villages. It would be a massacre.

Cornstalk addressed the assembled chiefs. "Shall we turn and fight them?" he asked, according to non-Indian traders on the scene. "Shall we kill our squaws and children and then fight until we are killed ourselves?" The chiefs were silent. Then Cornstalk sank his hatchet into the war post at the center of the council site. "Since you are not inclined to fight," he said, "I will make peace."

Rather than confront the leader of the settlers' militia, Cornstalk chose to meet with the territory's English governor at Camp Charlotte. No written record was made of the meeting, and afterward the two sides gave different accounts of what was agreed upon. The non-Indians claimed that Cornstalk had accepted the Stanwix boundary and surrendered Shawnee rights to the tribe's Kentucky hunting ground. The Shawnees said they had done no such thing but had only agreed to a truce. No matter what was decided at Camp Charlotte, however, settlers were soon back in Kentucky, and Indians were raiding to drive them out.

When Chiksika returned to his village with his father's body, he must have described the Point Pleasant battle to his mother and siblings. Their reaction will never be known; neither Tecumseh nor any other family member ever commented publicly on Pucksinwah's death. But it is reasonable to assume that it had a devastating effect, perhaps setting a suddenly fatherless, six-year-old Shawnee boy on the path of a lifelong crusade.

3

WARRIOR

After Pucksinwah's death, 16-year-old Chiksika stepped into the role of family hunter and provider. Black Fish, a war chief from a nearby village, also helped support Methotasa's household, as did her neighbors; caring for the families of fallen warriors was a community duty. Still, there were hard times.

The Shawnees did not give up claims to their Kentucky hunting grounds after Point Pleasant, and warriors continued their raids. To protect themselves from the attacks, the settlers built log forts, sturdy enclosures that were relatively easy to defend and made the settlers' lives easier—and longer. By the mid-1770s, Kentucky's non-Indian population had grown to more than 10,000 people.

In 1775, the situation in the Old Northwest grew more complicated with the outbreak of the American Revolution, the war by which the 13 American colonies won their independence from England. Although Indians in the Ohio Valley generally sided with the British—reliable trading partners who offered objects of value in return for what they wanted—most of the Shawnees chose to watch the war from the sidelines. Leading the Shawnee neutrality faction was Cornstalk, the chief who had gained his people's deep respect by demonstrating valor at Point Pleasant and wisdom in the negotiations that followed.

Fishing along a riverbank, a young Indian takes aim with an arrow, tied to his bow for easy retrieval. Bringing in fish and game for the tribe was among the duties of Tecumseh and other Shawnee males.

Steering a cautious middle course, Cornstalk met with both British and American representatives. He reassured the Americans of his support for the Camp Charlotte truce; at the same time, he appeared open to the British suggestion that his people join the war against the Americans. Although Cornstalk committed no warriors, his attitude encouraged the British to continue trading with the Shawnees.

Cornstalk kept up the appearance of neutrality as long as he could, but a large number of his tribe's young firebrands—including Tecumseh's brother Chiksika—lacked the old chief's patience. Tired of being kept from retaliating for the Americans' constant thefts of their land and murders of their people, these young warriors began a series of devastating attacks on settlers in Kentucky.

Cornstalk at last decided that, under these circumstances, neutrality was impossible. But he had signed the Camp Charlotte treaty, guaranteeing that he and his people would keep the peace. Before he abandoned the treaty and joined the British, Cornstalk felt obliged to tell the Americans. Accordingly, in October 1777, he called on Captain Matthew Arbuckle, commander of Fort Douglas on the Ohio River.

Arbuckle responded by throwing Cornstalk, along with the two warriors who had accompanied him, into jail. The Indians, he suspected, could be easily dealt with if he held their leader hostage. He never had time to find out. Within the hour, a mob of furious, heavily armed settlers galloped up to the fort and demanded to see Cornstalk. Arbuckle protested; the Shawnee and his men were unarmed, he said, and under U.S. protection.

Ignoring the captain, the lynch mob broke into Cornstalk's cell. The chief faced them calmly. "You may kill me if you please," he told them. "I can die but once, and it's all one to me now or at another time." The mob murdered Cornstalk and his companions without further conversation.

Outraged by the killing, the other Shawnee chiefs now joined the British. Black Fish and Black Hoof led their warriors on raids south into the Kentucky settlements and as far east as Virginia's Shenandoah Valley, burning farms and wreaking havoc as they went. The Americans, who were busy fighting a revolution in the East, were forced to raise troops for a counterstrike against the Indians in the West.

Many Shawnees were deeply disturbed by the prospect of a long war, which would bring legions of vengeful settlers sweeping into their villages. In the past, the Shawnees had often migrated when conditions in their homeland grew threatening, and in the spring of 1779, some decided it was time to move again. Among this group was Methotasa. Taking her youngest daughter, she joined a band of some 1,000 Shawnees and went to live in southern Missouri. She left the rest of her family with the tribe along the Little Miami River, under the guardianship of Black Fish, Pucksinwah's old comrade in arms.

Most of Tecumseh's immediate family, including his beloved oldest sister, Tecumapese, stayed behind. Tecumapese was married to Wasegoboah, a respected warrior, and the couple welcomed Tecumseh to their household. The separation of relatives was not unusual among the Shawnees, who were often more closely connected to neighbors and friends than to their immediate family members. Still, Tecumseh was only 11 years old when his mother moved away; perhaps it occurred to him that the Shawnees' troubles with the non-Indian world had now cost him both his parents.

Those troubles would soon cost him even more. In May, shortly after Methotasa and the others left for the

South, a Kentucky militia unit attacked the Shawnee village of Chillicothe, home of Black Fish. That day, the Americans' losses were heavier than those of the Indians, but Black Fish received a mortal wound and died a week later.

The death of his guardian left young Tecumseh in grief but not in despair. A handsome youth, wiry and well-muscled, he was a leader among the boys of the village, as befitted the son of a great war chief. He had become an excellent shot with both musket and bow and

A traveling French artist produced this somewhat romanticized portrait of a Shawnee warrior in the late 18th century. All young Shawnee males learned to ride and handle weapons, but Tecumseh, an outstanding horseman and a bowman of deadly accuracy, easily outshone his peers.

often led his friends on hunting trips in the forest. Even as a boy, Tecumseh seemed to possess a certain charisma: He "always had a set of followers," one admirer recalled, "who were ready to stand and fall with him."

The Shawnees taught their boys to become fearless men. Except in extreme cases, they believed that punishing boys stifled their manliness, and neither Tecumseh nor his friends were rebuked for misbehavior, even for displays of aggression against others or for damaging tribal property. As a Shawnee boy grew up, he received instruction from the warriors and hunters, or if they were absent, from the elderly men of the village. The old taught the young by telling stories of the glorious hunts, raiding parties, and other adventures of their youth.

Shawnees placed a high value on the art of speech-making. Orators who could hold a village spellbound with words were believed to possess greatness. As a boy, Tecumseh heard some of the Shawnees' most outstanding storytellers, including his own father, Pucksinwah; Cornstalk; and Black Fish. In years to come, non-Indians would be regularly amazed by the remarkable power of Tecumseh's oratory, as well as by his mastery of Shawnee social and political history. Both his extensive knowledge of tribal history and his dazzling speechmaking were rooted in the days when, in silent awe, he had listened to his people's great storytellers.

Shawnee boys had to learn the arts of war and of the hunt. On both fronts, Tecumseh relied on his brother Chiksika, his senior by 12 years. Chiksika, who had served in combat beside their revered father and who was now a strong hunter and warrior in his own right, had much to teach the boy. Tecumseh idolized him, and he returned his younger brother's affection, taking him on far-off hunting trips that sometimes lasted for weeks or even months. Tecumseh's clan, the Kispokotha, had a long tradition of producing war chiefs, and the boy himself came from a family of warriors. Tecumseh was thus well positioned to learn the arts of war. Some scholars believe that he first experienced battle at the age of 14.

According to these historians, Tecumseh had followed his war-chief brother, Chiksika, into a 1782 battle against a band of invading Kentucky militiamen. After being pursued by the soldiers along the Licking River, the Shawnees had regrouped at a narrow ravine near Blue Licks, waited for the Kentuckians, then ambushed them. In the fierce fighting that followed, Chiksika was slightly wounded. Tecumseh was frightened almost out of his wits.

Encircled by a ring of huge, bearded militiamen, the young Shawnee is said to have taken to his heels and run for miles before stopping to realize what he had done—deserted. Then he shamefacedly returned to camp and told his brother he was ready to receive his punishment. To what must have been the boy's vast relief, Chiksika and the tribe's elders said that fear in battle was acceptable—*once*. If Tecumseh never repeated the performance, he could remain an honorable Shawnee. Whether the story is accurate or not, one fact is beyond doubt: no one, friend or enemy, ever accused the Shawnee warrior Tecumseh of cowardice.

And on the frontier, courage was an indispensable commodity. It was especially needed during the American Revolution, when torture and mutilation became common coin. Both Indians and whites committed acts of almost unimaginable barbarity. Two incidents will, perhaps, suggest the horror of those days. The first took place in 1782 at Gnadenhutten, a village of peaceful Christian Delaware Indians on the Tuscarawas River, in eastern Ohio.

Suspecting the Gnadenhutten Indians of spying for the British, Colonel David Williamson and a company of Pennsylvania militia invaded the village and rounded up

Pennsylvania militiamen slaughter 96 unarmed Delaware children, women, and men at the village of Gnadenhutten. A witness to the 1782 massacre later recalled a soldier who killed 14 Indians with a mallet, then said to a comrade: "My arm fails me. Go on in the same way. I think I have done pretty well." The carnage led to bloody Indian reprisals.

its 34 children and 62 adults, many of whom were kneeling in prayer at the time. The soldiers bound the Indians hand and foot, smashed their skulls with mallets, scalped them, then burned their bodies.

Pleased with their "victory" over the suspected spies, the Pennsylvanians decided to wipe out another Delaware village. But the second campaign worked out differently. As 480 soldiers—this time commanded not by Williamson but by Colonel William Crawford—approached their target, they marched straight into an ambush: 1,000 Delaware and Wyandot Indians, eager to revenge Gnadenhutten, pounced on the column and tore it to pieces. Among the 11 whites captured by the Indians was Colonel Crawford.

All the prisoners were sentenced to death. The colonel, who had taken no part in the murders at Gnadenhutten but who was judged guilty of them anyway, was condemned to die in particular agony. The Indians stripped him, beat him savagely, then peppered his wounds with gunpowder. After that, they cut off his ears and gradually roasted him over a fire as relatives of the Gnadenhutten victims looked on approvingly.

Tecumseh had his own views on the custom of torturing prisoners. About a year after the Indians revenged Gnadenhutten, he and other Shawnee warriors attacked a convoy of supply-laden American flatboats on the Ohio River. During the battle, Tecumseh killed four men, more than any of the older, seasoned warriors. The 15-year-old had behaved, his companions later noted, "with great bravery," outshining "some of the oldest and bravest warriors." By the time the fighting ended, the Indians had killed all but one of the white men.

Without even discussing their next move, the victorious Shawnees built a fire and burned their prisoner at the stake. As he screamed in agony, the warriors encircling him screamed, too—with delighted, mocking laughter at their victim's death throes. Tecumseh, who had never taken part in torturing an enemy, felt a deep sense of revulsion and shame at his tribesmen's actions. But the grisly practice was well established, and both sides often committed similar atrocities. The young warrior's next move, therefore, was remarkable.

Addressing the war party, which included his brother Chiksika, Tecumseh denounced the practice of torturing helpless men. An enemy should of course be killed, he said, but as a man, not "as a rat cornered and tied and burned alive." The older warriors reacted with anger and puzzlement, but Tecumseh continued: burning a man at the stake was the work of cowards, he said, a work that insulted the spirit of Moneto, the supreme being.

Tecumseh spoke passionately and at some length. When he finished, he offered his knife to Red Horse, the warrior who had been most outraged at his revolutionary words. Red Horse, said Tecumseh, should take the knife and kill him if he had not spoken the truth. Astonishingly,

Red Horse refused the weapon and said he now agreed with Tecumseh; he would continue to kill men in battle, but he would never again torture a prisoner. One by one, the other warriors made the same vow, in a few minutes ending a practice as old as the Shawnee tribe itself. Tecumseh had taken another step on his unique road.

With the 1783 Treaty of Paris, the war between England and the United States ended, but the war between settlers and western Indians continued to rage. During the American Revolution, the Indians had managed to hold the settlers south of the Ohio River, but after 1783, new settlements began cropping up along the north banks of the river. Mingo and Cherokee warriors retaliated with a string of raids in Kentucky.

Although the Shawnees took no part in these attacks, Kentuckians blamed them and sent their militias to raid

Delawares and Wyandots revenge Gnadenhutten with the torture and killing of Pennsylvania militia colonel William Crawford. Traditional for centuries, such barbaric practices were not only condoned but cheered by Indians of both sexes and all ages.

the Shawnee villages along the Miami River. Burning crops, destroying villages, and slaughtering every Indian they saw, the soldiers cut a bloody swath through the valley. They were, in fact, so intent on revenge that they sometimes struck blindly; during a 1786 raid, militiamen shot a friendly Shawnee chief who had just ceded a huge tract of tribal land to the United States.

The Shawnees soon fought back, and when they did, Tecumseh saw action as a full-fledged warrior. In late 1787, when Chiksika led a war party toward Tennessee and Kentucky, his 19-year-old brother rode at his side. Traveling from one tribal village to another, the Shawnees offered help where it was needed: over the next year and a half, they battled alongside Miamis, Kickapoos, Sacs, Winnebagoes, and Cherokees. The tribes fought well together, perhaps giving Tecumseh his first ideas about the great Indian federation that would one day become his life's obsession.

In April 1789, the Shawnee war party visited a community of Tennessee Cherokees who had recently

Indians (barely visible at top of riverbank) attack a bargeload of fur traders on the Missouri River. It was after such an action that Tecumseh stood up to his fellow warriors, denounced the routine torture of prisoners, and forever changed his people's method of treating captured enemies.

suffered heavy losses from marauding soldiers. When the Cherokees asked the Shawnees to help them destroy the white raiders' fort, Chiksika and his men agreed at once. The night before the planned attack, the mood in the Shawnee camp was confident, and spirits ran high.

But just as Tecumseh finished laying out his battle gear, Chiksika approached him with chilling words. He had had a vision, he told his younger brother: at noon the next day, a bullet would strike him between the eyes, killing him instantly. Chiksika's prophecies had so often proved accurate that Tecumseh felt no doubts now; his heart was heavy.

The battle, Chiksika went on to say, should not end with his death. Victory would belong to the Shawnees and Cherokees if they continued to fight. He said that Tecumseh should lead them and that he would one day become a great leader, not only of the Shawnee nation but of all Indians. Tecumseh did not respond and made no effort to persuade his brother to stay out of the next day's battle. He knew Chiksika would never run from his fate.

In the morning, the Indians charged the fort three times. Each time, the whites' fire drove them back, but each time, the Indians picked off more soldiers. At noon, they were preparing for their fourth charge when Tecumseh heard a single rifle shot from the fort. He reached Chiksika just as he slipped from his saddle dead, a bullet hole in the center of his forehead.

Remembering his brother's words about continuing the battle, Tecumseh waved his war club and urged the Cherokees and Shawnees on. Chiksika's death, however, struck them as an evil omen, and they withdrew, abandoning an almost certain victory. As Tecumseh gathered up his brother's lifeless body, he dropped the war club, which Chiksika had given him years earlier. He would soon raise it again.

4

WAR CHIEF

After Chiksika's death, most of the Shawnee warriors returned home, but Tecumseh and a few others continued raiding. Along with Cherokee and Creek warriors, they battled the Long Knives in Tennessee, Kentucky, Alabama, and even in far-off Florida. Historians know little about Tecumseh's life during this period, but it is certain that he was profoundly grieved by the loss of his beloved brother and mentor. It may have been his desire to avenge Chiksika that kept him on the warpath long after others had left it.

Tecumseh, who had joined the war party as Chiksika's follower, was now leading the warriors. Like most Indian battle groups, Tecumseh's raiders practiced what would later be called guerrilla warfare: silently prowling the woods, they carefully selected a target, noted its vulnerable points, and waited. Choosing a moment when the settlers were off guard, the warriors charged out of the forest with blood-chilling war whoops, swinging tomahawks and firing rifles. After killing settlers and setting fires, they melted back into the forest, disappearing until they reemerged to besiege the next hapless community. Taking scalps, wreaking havoc, and spreading terror, the Indians haunted the frontier.

A Kentucky-bound settler rests his mules on the Wilderness Road, a trail blazed by frontiersman Daniel Boone through the Cumberland Gap. As non-Indians pressed west in ever-increasing numbers, they cleared forests, fenced fields, caught fish, and hunted game, all of which had belonged to the land's Indian residents for hundreds of years.

After scalping his partner, Indians capture frontier road builder James Smith in 1745. Despite unremitting Indian hostility, a steady stream of settlers poured into Kentucky; by the time Tecumseh was 17, in 1785, more than 40,000 whites had migrated to the land they called Heaven on Earth.

Still, the settlers kept coming. By 1785, more than 40,000 whites had migrated to Kentucky, and thousands more were moving in north of the Ohio River. Between 1785 and 1790, some 20,000 non-Indians entered the Ohio Valley. These settlers wanted the U.S. government to end the Indians' violence permanently by waging an all-out war against them. But raising troops and equipping an army was a costly enterprise, and the young U.S. government was strapped for funds.

But President George Washington knew that even in peace, the Indians would not take the government seriously unless it maintained at least a token military presence. In 1790, he persuaded Congress to establish a federal army of 1,216 officers and men, most of them to be sent to the West. The president also instructed Arthur St. Clair, governor of the Northwest Territory, to raise 1,500 additional militiamen from Kentucky and Pennsylvania for frontier duty. Washington hoped that the mere presence of the troops would intimidate the Indians and lead them to accept new American offers of money for land.

But some Indians were in no mood to listen to such offers. Because the militia had all but destroyed the Shawnee villages along the Little Miami, the Shawnees had moved their villages yet again. This time, they had settled even farther to the north and west, in the region along the Maumee River, in what is now northwest Ohio. The main Shawnee villages were now near towns of the Miami, Wyandot, and Ottawa Indians. These tribes and others worked with the Shawnees to build an alliance against the Americans.

The tribes were all opposed to American expansion, but they could not agree on just where the settlers ought to be stopped. The disputes among Indians made it easier for the Americans to negotiate their dubious treaties of the 1780s. They always seemed able to find some Indians willing to sign away land—with or without the approval of its inhabitants. But in 1790, when Governor St. Clair sent messengers to the Miami villages with proposals for a peace conference, the Miamis threatened to kill the messengers. The Shawnees proved similarly uncooperative.

Deciding to teach the Miamis and Shawnees a lesson, St. Clair dispatched soldiers and militia to their villages. Explaining that he wished to achieve the "humbling and chastising [of] some of the savage tribes," St. Clair told a British officer of his move. No friend of the Americans, the officer warned the Indians about the invasion, and when the American troops, commanded by General Josiah Harmar, arrived at the Indian villages, he found them deserted. Meanwhile, Shawnee scouts were secretly tracking the militia's every move.

The troops had no choice but to search out their enemy. Marching through the woods, unaware that they were being watched, they were easy targets. The Indians ambushed the column twice, sending militiamen fleeing in fear each time. In two days of fighting, nearly 200 invaders and about 100 Indians were killed. Harmar's men had done damage, burning the Shawnee fields and destroying some 20,000 bushels of corn, but the engagements were still clear victories for the Indians.

When Tecumseh and his warriors returned to the Shawnee villages in November 1790, his people were still overjoyed with their recent successes in battle. They now seemed confident that they could eventually defeat the Long Knives. They would soon put themselves to the test again.

In January 1791, the Shawnee warriors headed south once more, raiding forts and villages and bushwhacking river boats carrying new settlers and supplies. Tecumseh, now a proven war chief experienced at leading men into combat, was among the raiders. The Americans soon prepared a counterattack, this time to be led by Governor St. Clair himself. He assembled some 2,300 men at Cincinnati, but preparations were slow. His troops were not ready to leave their base until October 4.

As the troops marched sluggishly toward the Maumee River communities, about 150 miles to the north, Tecumseh and a small party of scouts tracked them. Plagued by cold, rainy weather and desertions, the army covered only a few miles each day; after about a month, the soldiers had traveled only 80 miles. On November 3, they made camp on the east bank of the Wabash River, near the current Indiana-Ohio state line.

Just before dawn on November 4, as the still-drowsy soldiers were building their breakfast fires, shrieking warriors burst upon them from three directions. The noise, soldiers later recalled, sounded like the "howling of thousands of wolves." The warriors had taken the soldiers completely by surprise. As soldiers panicked and ran helter-skelter about the camp, the Indians cut them down with hatchets and knives.

By 9 A.M., the attack was over. The bodies of soldiers lay everywhere in the camp. Meanwhile, to the south, some 500 surviving soldiers were fleeing "like a drove of bullocks," as one of them later recalled. Toward the front of the retreating herd, mounted on a pack horse, was Governor St. Clair himself. The army had suffered 647 dead and 271 wounded; the Indians, 21 dead and 40 wounded. This Wabash River battle still ranks as the most one-sided defeat ever inflicted on the U.S. Army.

In the spring of 1792, the United States began to rebuild its shattered army. Partly to buy time for this task, the government sent an Iroquois intermediary to the Indians with a new peace offer. The Americans said they were willing to establish a boundary line along the Muskingum River, leaving all lands to the west and north—except for tracts already inhabited by settlers—to the tribes.

As one team member navigates the canoe, the other lands the quarry. Said to be very effective, the torch-fishing technique was widely practiced by the Indians of the Old Northwest.

Arthur St. Clair, governor of the Northwest Territory from 1787 until 1802, had served the United States with distinction, first as a general during the American Revolution, then as president of the Continental Congress. His shining record was tarnished, however, when he went up against Tecumseh in late 1791; the Wabash River battle still holds the record as the U.S. Army's most stunning defeat.

Messquakenoe, a Shawnee chief, scoffed at this offer. The Americans, he said, had lost the last contest with the Indians; they had no business offering peace terms. The Shawnees, however, *would* offer terms: in exchange for peace, said Messquakenoe, the United States would recognize that all land north of the Ohio River belonged to Indians and that settlers living there must withdraw. The Americans also had to reimburse the Shawnees for stealing the tribe's Kentucky hunting grounds.

Recognizing an impossible situation when he saw one, the Iroquois intermediary did not even bother to report these terms to the Americans. He merely said that the tribes were prepared to talk peace the following year. To the United States, this was a clear rejection of its terms; the nation began preparing for war. Congress quickly authorized the recruitment of more than 5,000 soldiers and appropriated more than $1 million—a truly massive sum in 1792—to pay and supply them. To command this army, President Washington appointed Major General Anthony Wayne, a legendary Revolutionary War hero known as Mad Anthony.

Wayne was a dashing soldier, but despite his nickname he was also a careful planner. He was determined to learn from the mistakes of Harmar and St. Clair. In early 1793, the government told the Indians it was ready to present a new peace offer—but at the same time, Wayne garrisoned his troops at Fort Washington, near Cincinnati. Understandably, the Shawnees were suspicious. If the United States wanted peace, they asked, why had it stationed a large new army at Fort Washington?

Insisting that the army was for defensive purposes only, the government outlined a new peace offer, but the Indians rejected it as blatantly unfair. Months of wrangling followed, leading no closer to an end to hostilities. At last, in September 1793, Wayne and his troops—more than 4,000 men, including a large contingent of Kentucky sharpshooters—started marching west. The Indians were ready for the Long Knives, but they soon saw that Wayne's tough, dependable regulars were a far cry from the raw, undisciplined forces led by Harmar and St. Clair.

Wayne's army covered a good 10 miles on a day's march. And, unlike Harmar and St. Clair, Wayne did not attack in the autumn when the Indians were rested and well-supplied but chose his moment carefully. Impressed with his guile and cunning, Shawnee scouts began calling him Sukachgook—the Black Snake.

While the Indians were waiting to confront Wayne, Lord Dorchester, the British governor of Canada, made a surprising announcement. He said he expected his country to be at war with the United States within a year. He also led the Indians to believe that when Black Snake attacked, they could count on assistance from their old allies, the British. Meanwhile, British officials stationed in Canada built themselves a military post. Their Fort Miami was situated near present-day Toledo, Ohio, well within the United States border.

Wayne's army moved methodically, building forts as it went; new American outposts soon studded the embattled frontier. As the army approached the Shawnee and Miami villages, their residents fled; the soldiers burned the deserted dwellings and trampled the crops. Soon afterward, on August 20, 1794, a war party led by the Shawnee chief Blue Jacket concealed itself about five miles upstream from the British Fort Miami. The area they selected, known as Fallen Timbers, seemed ideal for their purpose. Some years earlier, a tornado had ploughed a path through the forest, twisting the fallen trees into a perfect trap for advancing troops.

There, at Fallen Timbers, the Indians waited to do battle with Wayne's troops, confident that if a retreat became necessary, they could take refuge inside the British Fort Miami. The warriors lined up in a crescent-shaped formation, planning to lure the troops deep into the field, then close in around them. Once again, however, the Indians betrayed themselves by a lapse in discipline. Just as the soldiers came into view, but before they were near enough to be surrounded, the Ottawas charged out after them, whooping and swinging their hatchets. The element of surprise was lost.

The other warriors, confused by the Ottawas, also leaped into the fray. At first, the soldiers seemed to panic, just as the troops of Harmar and St. Clair had done. Then into the midst of the battle galloped Mad Anthony Wayne himself, shouting orders to stand and fight—and promising to shoot any man who did not.

The soldiers quickly began driving the disorganized warriors back. The Indian war party was saved from total slaughter by the stout resistance of the Wyandots and

"Charge!" roars General Anthony Wayne at Fallen Timbers, Ohio. Despite ferocious resistance by Tecumseh and other warriors, "Mad Anthony" took just 40 minutes to win the 1794 battle, a victory that would lead to the Indian surrender of hundreds of thousands of acres north of the Ohio River.

Shawnees: Tecumseh and his men battled fiercely at the forefront, holding off the soldiers while other warriors retreated. During the intense fighting, however, Tecumseh's younger brother Sauwaseekau was slain.

The warriors fleeing the battle headed south to Fort Miami. They expected the British to protect them, but when they arrived, they found the gates bolted. From behind the walls, a British officer shouted that any Indian who tried to enter would be shot. Despite Dorchester's earlier assurances, the British feared that if they were seen openly aiding the Indians, they might drag their nation into an unwanted war with the United States.

The Battle of Fallen Timbers was a decisive victory for the U.S. government. Driven from their villages, defeated in the field, and abandoned by their allies, the Indians now found themselves in desperate straits.

5

THE OPEN DOOR

The Indians had few options after their defeat at Fallen Timbers. Without British aid, it was useless to keep fighting the Americans, whose troops were better equipped, better disciplined, and more numerous. Nor could the Indians simply return to what remained of their villages, which now lay in the shadows of American forts.

By mid-September 1794, the beaten warriors and their families had slowly made their way to the eastern shore of Lake Erie, where they set up a ragged camp near the mouth of the Maumee River. Supplies were scarce; without the food donated by sympathetic British Indian agents, many of the 2,500 refugees might have starved that winter. Not surprisingly, then, when Wayne's messengers arrived at the Lake Erie camp with a peace offer, they found most of the Indians ready to listen.

To receive the American peace terms, 1,100 chiefs and warriors convened at General Wayne's headquarters in Greenville that summer. The terms were harsh: the United States would take possession of about two-thirds of what is now the state of Ohio, a huge slice of Indiana, and several large tracts of land inside the acreage allotted to the Indians. And the new American forts in Indian territory would stay put.

Those who knew Tecumseh called this portrait, drawn by a French trader, the best likeness of him ever made. The Shawnee leader had little interest in posing for artists, forcing most of those who depicted him to rely on memory or friends' descriptions.

In August 1795, 91 chiefs from 12 nations in the Ohio Valley and lower Great Lakes put their marks on the Treaty of Greenville. In return for the vast sweep of land that had been their birthright, the Indians—*collectively*—were to receive $20,000 immediately and $9,500 each year thereafter. These sums were to be paid not in money but in goods, the cash value of which would be set by the United States.

Wayne had made it clear he would view failure to participate in the Greenville council as an unfriendly gesture: Tecumseh refused even to appear. He also refused to follow federal regulations. By government order, Indians could hunt in their old territory only until settlers came. Defiantly, Tecumseh took a small group of followers and moved to Deer Creek, an area of southern Ohio already populated with settlers. The Shawnee warrior had no intention of living in any of the Shawnee villages near the American forts. He and his people moved often, following the good hunting. Sometimes, they cleared fields, planted crops, and stayed in one spot until harvest time, then moved on once more.

Not much is known of Tecumseh's personal life, but stories abound. One of them involves Rebecca Galloway, daughter of a white farmer in Ohio. When he was in his thirties, Tecumseh is said to have formed a deep attachment to the blond, blue-eyed young woman, who took it upon herself to educate the tall, commanding young warrior. According to some historians, Galloway introduced Tecumseh to the great works of English literature, to the Bible, and to the history of the Old World and the New. He is said to have asked her to marry him and to have received her acceptance—but only if he gave up his Indian ways and lived as a white man. After considering her terms for some weeks, Tecumseh declined. He could never abandon his people, he told her, not even for love.

Hunters, one armed with bow and arrow, the other with a rifle, close in on a pair of buffalo, the most important element in the western tribes' survival. Killing only the animals they needed, Indians coexisted with the West's immense herds for centuries, but settlers shot buffalo for sport, effectively exterminating them in a few decades.

Whether that story is true or not, it is beyond doubt that Tecumseh married twice. In 1794, he wed Mohnetohse, a Peckuwe woman who reportedly became shrill and dictatorial as soon as the wedding was over. After she bore him a son, Tecumseh sent her away, much to the approval of his friends. He took the boy, Mahyawwekawpawe, to live with his sister, Tecumapese.

Tecumseh's followers urged him to set a good example by taking another wife, and a year later, he did, this one an older woman whose warrior husband had recently died. Mamate, the second wife, gave him another son, then died of complications from childbirth. Her infant, whom Tecumseh named Naythawaynah (A Panther Seizing its Prey), also went to live with Tecumapese, a generous woman who loved children. Tecumseh's political activities seem to have left him little time to spend with the boys, about whom scholars have unearthed few facts.

In 1800, Tecumseh went to live along the White River, near present-day Indianapolis. He and his followers, by then numbering more than 100 people, tried to live in traditional tribal style, sustaining themselves on the game from the forests and crops from the Midwest's fertile soil. The inescapable presence of settlers, however, served as a constant reminder that things were not as they once had been.

Almost before the ink on the Greenville Treaty had dried, Americans started scheming to get the lands promised to the tribes. Unable to support themselves, Indians in the fort towns grew to depend on American annuity payments and loans. Officials encouraged these Indians to borrow heavily, knowing they would be forced to sell their remaining lands to pay their debts. William Henry Harrison, new governor of Indiana Territory, was among those who perfected this land-acquisition strategy. By 1806, Harrison, representing the United States, had bought or been granted title to some 70 million acres of land on the Indian side of the Greenville Treaty line.

The tribal villages near the forts gradually declined into shantytowns, beset by poverty, disease, and despair. The Indians' proximity to whites exposed them to illnesses to which they had no immunity; hundreds died from smallpox, whooping cough, and influenza. A large number of others, demoralized by unemployment and constant loss of their homes, began abusing alcohol, always readily available from American traders. Many Indian women fought poverty by selling themselves as prostitutes to soldiers and settlers.

The once-valiant chiefs of the Old Northwest Indians had betrayed their people for bribes; now, those in search of leadership looked elsewhere. Many turned to Tecumseh. As the years wore on and the promises of Greenville proved increasingly hollow, the memory of his refusal to

Traveling in their customary manner—men and boys on horseback, women and girls on foot—a group of Shawnees crosses the plains as Tecumseh and his followers did in 1800. The tribe carries its possessions by travois, *a traditional Shawnee vehicle consisting of two trailing poles and a platform or net for the load.*

attend the treaty talks enhanced his stature. Indians were inspired by his independence, courage, and pride. Even whites appreciated his outstanding qualities and often sought his aid and counsel.

When southern Ohio settlers grew alarmed about Shawnee hunting and camping in the fall of 1799, white authorities summoned Tecumseh. In calm, well-chosen words, the young war chief assured the settlers that the Indians meant no harm, thus defusing a potentially explosive situation. In 1803, Tecumseh was again asked to quell tensions on the frontier. This time, the crisis began with the murder of a homesteader. Certain that

Indians had committed the crime, a group of vigilantes had retaliated by murdering Wawwilaway, an elderly Shawnee who had expressed friendship for whites. When news of Wawwilaway's murder spread, whites expected an Indian uprising. Settlers called for militia and began fleeing their homes in panic.

White officials invited Tecumseh to address settlers in Chillicothe. He told them that none of his people were involved in the murder of the homesteader. Nevertheless, he said, the Shawnees would not seek vengeance for Wawwilaway's lynching; the old man had taken care of it himself by killing one of his attackers just before he died. Enough blood had been spilled, said Tecumseh, and the matter was best forgotten. A militia captain who heard him speak at Chillicothe called the war chief "one of the most dignified men I ever beheld." His "noble bearing," added the captain, "dispelled as if by magic the apprehensions of the whites."

But Tecumseh's message to the whites of Chillicothe went beyond soothing words. He also warned them to keep their promise not to bother Indians west of the Greenville Treaty line. More and more young warriors began looking to him for leadership; many left their villages to join his. They saw in him a remnant of a lost time, a time when their leaders were brave and noble hunters and warriors, not cringing favor seekers.

Tecumseh may have represented what was good in the past, but his younger brother surely personified much of what was wrong with the present. Lowawluwaysica was one of the triplets born two years after Tecumseh. The Shawnees believed that any individual born in a set of triplets would lead a remarkable life, but unfortunately, the only thing remarkable about young Lowawluwaysica was his lack of loveable qualities. He was also clumsy in games, a fault considered grave by the Shawnees. Playing with a bow and arrow as a boy, Lowawluwaysica accidently pierced his right eye, blinding it for life and deforming the right side of his face.

Nicknamed Rattler for his bragging, overbearing ways, Lowawluwaysica inspired little sympathy for his misfortunes. By the time he was a teenager, he had begun to drink heavily, and he proved a poor hunter and provider for his family. But the most disgraceful thing about Lowawluwaysica, in the eyes of his people, was that he never grew to be a warrior, never entered the field of battle for his nation. Although he did join his brothers at Fallen Timbers, he was said to have run away before the battle started.

Having failed at various Shawnee callings, Lowawluwaysica settled down to become an apprentice to Penagushea, the medicine man of the White River camp. The older man taught Lowawluwaysica the tribal arts of ministering to both the body and the mind. After Penagushea died in late 1804, Lowawluwaysica tested his new healing skills during an influenza epidemic, trying traditional medicines made from roots and herbs, magical incantations, even prayers. Nothing worked. The epidemic got worse and many died.

Lowawluwaysica's mood darkened after the failure of his medicine, and he began to drink even more heavily. Then, one evening as he sat by his fire, he collapsed on the floor and sank into a deep sleep. All night and into the next day, he lay motionless. After a while, detecting no signs of life in him, his wife began to prepare for his funeral. As she did so, Lowawluwaysica suddenly woke up and told a strange story. He had gone through an experience quite like death, he said. During this period, his soul had been taken to the dwelling of the Great Spirit, who selected him to carry a message to the Great Spirit's children, the Indians.

Shawnee chief Black Hoof was highly regarded by his people, but he lost the respect of many, especially Tecumseh, when he signed the Treaty of Greenville in 1779. "Dogs and skunks have not so little mind as those who did this," said Tecumseh. "Every Indian who has put his thumb to it should have his thumbs cut off!"

This message, which Lowawluwaysica now revealed, was that the Great Spirit felt sorrowful because his red children had started behaving in the manner of whites, who were created by evil spirits. If Indians wished to protect themselves, and win back the Great Spirit's favor, they were to throw off white influences such as woven cloth, wheat bread, the flesh of domestic animals, and—especially—alcohol. Warriors were to shave their heads and wear, as their forefathers had, scalp locks. They were to hunt with bows instead of guns, although they could continue to use guns against whites.

Befitting his status as divine messenger, said Lowa-wluwaysica, the Great Spirit had given him a new name: Tenskwatawa, which means "The Open Door." He said it would be his mission to show Indians how to follow the Great Spirit in this world, so they would be ready for the good life in the next world. Preaching to receptive listeners of various tribes, Tenskwatawa quickly won numerous followers who believed that this former drunkard had been transformed into a holy man. He soon became known as the Prophet.

Did Tecumseh, too, believe in his brother's vision? Scholars and historians have long debated this question. Some see a clear connection between Tenskwatawa's prophetic message and Tecumseh's political ideas; Tecumseh, they suggest, invented the message, then persuaded his younger brother to publicize it. Others believe that Tenskwatawa was sincere about his vision but that Tecumseh never believed in it.

In any case, Tecumseh and Tenskwatawa worked closely together. In 1805, they moved with their followers to Greenville, Ohio, where they erected a village and settled down. It was the most defiant gesture either man had ever made: Greenville was on U.S. territory, off limits to Indians. It was also the site of Anthony Wayne's former headquarters and of the negotiations for the hated Treaty of Greenville. By moving to this particular location, the Shawnee brothers were thumbing their noses at the U.S. government.

6

▼▼▼

"ASK HIM TO CAUSE THE SUN TO STAND STILL"

Tenskwatawa wears his full prophet's regalia in this portrait by frontier artist George Catlin. When the Prophet strode onto an Ohio meadow on June 16, 1806, he ordered the sun to darken— and it did. He had known that a solar eclipse would occur, but to his dazzled followers, his performance proved that he was the Great Spirit's messenger.

Soon after the Shawnee brothers and their followers built their new village at Greenville, Tenskwatawa—the Prophet—began spreading his message to the area's tribal towns. He preached electrifying sermons on the evils of white practices, especially the drinking of alcohol, and urged Indians to return to the ways of their forefathers. When they did, he said, their lands would be restored, and the white men banished from their midst.

The Prophet won a host of converts; he also loosed a wave of violence. He identified all who opposed him as "witches," and said they must be reeducated—or eliminated. The worst of them, the Prophet maintained, were Indians who took the road traveled by whites, those children of "the great serpent." In one Delaware village, Tenskwatawa presided over the torture and execution of five so-called witches accused of "living white." According to some reports, Tenskwatawa's witch-hunts horrified his brother, who threatened to kill him unless he stopped.

When Governor Harrison heard about Tenskwatawa's activities, he scolded the Delawares for heeding "this pretended prophet who dares to speak in the name of the Great Creator." The Indians, advised Harrison, should make Tenskwatawa prove he was God's messenger by

A trader puts his customers in a receptive mood by distributing necklaces, mirrors, and other small gifts. Intrigued with such sparkling items, Indians were often swindled by fast-talking merchants, particularly in the case of land sales.

performing a miracle. "If he is really a prophet, ask of him to cause the sun to stand still," Harrison said, "or the dead to rise from their graves."

Harrison hoped to expose Tenskwatawa as a fraud, but his demand did just the opposite. Accepting the challenge, the Prophet announced that, at Greenville on June 16, 1806, he would make the sun stand still and turn day into night. Eager to witness such a feat, a vast crowd of Indians assembled in Greenville on the appointed day. They watched from a distance as Tenskwatawa, standing alone in a field, raised his hand toward the heavens. Incredibly, the sun seemed to stop and darken. In the middle of the day, night fell; in the Greenville field, the crowd stood in awed silence.

Most of the whites understood that what they had just observed was a total eclipse of the sun. Officials tried to explain to the Indians that Tenskwatawa had merely learned that the eclipse was due—any farmer's almanac would have listed the information—and then performed his "miracle" at the appropriate time.

But the Indians at Greenville found the Prophet's dramatic performance far more impressive than the officials' explanations. They now believed that Tenskwatawa was truly the Great Spirit's messenger, holding power over the sun itself. When word of his great feat spread among the tribes, Indian pilgrims flocked to Greenville.

Many came armed and in a defiant antiwhite mood, prompting alarmed U.S. officials to send Tecumseh and Tenskwatawa a message in April 1807. The Indian settlement at Greenville, they said, showed disrespect for the United States and must be vacated. Tecumseh replied tersely. The Master of Life, he said, "has appointed this place for us to light our fires, and here we will remain."

Tension continued to rise. When a settler was murdered near the Little Miami River in the summer of 1807, whites instantly blamed it on Indians, and rumors of a coming war with the tribes swept the frontier settlements. Anxiety rose in July, when the crew of a British warship fired upon and boarded the U.S. frigate *Chesapeake* off Hampton Roads, Virginia. Many Americans feared that their old enemies, the British, would soon use the Indians—especially those "fanatics" camped at Greenville—to strike at the United States.

To calm the settlers' fears, Tecumseh accompanied a delegation of chiefs to Chillicothe, where he spoke for three hours. He promised that if whites lived up to the Greenville Treaty, his people would keep the peace, no matter what the English did. But he warned that Indians would give up no more land north of the Ohio River and that they would defend their remaining territory with their lives.

But even as Tecumseh was telling the settlers to honor the Greenville Treaty, the treaty had become a dead issue. By 1807, non-Indians had bought millions of acres west of the Greenville line, acquiring it from "government chiefs"—leaders who met with U.S. government approval. These land sales particularly infuriated the tribes' young warriors, who joined the pool of potential recruits for the Shawnee brothers. Only a united Indian front, the Shawnees insisted, could put a stop to such sales and protect the tribes' remaining land.

Although the brothers' message appealed to young warriors, the established chiefs often shunned it. In the autumn of 1807, however, Main Poche, a Potawatomi chief from Illinois and one of the most influential tribal leaders west of the Wabash River, paid a visit to Greenville. Main Poche agreed that Indians had to protect their remaining lands, but he was put off by talk of an intertribal union. His people had long waged war against other tribes, and he had no intention of uniting with his enemies. His reluctance was typical of older chiefs who otherwise supported the aims of the Shawnee brothers.

But as things turned out, Main Poche did assist the movement. Realizing that Greenville's poor hunting and meager harvests could not feed its swelling pilgrim population, he invited the Greenville Indians to move their camp to his people's territory. The site he offered, at the junction of the Wabash River and Tippecanoe River, promised better hunting and good fishing. Agreeing to the move, Tecumseh, Tenskwatawa, and their followers set out in the spring.

The Shawnee brothers soon built a village, which they named Prophetstown, on the northwest bank of the

As the Chesapeake's *mortally wounded Captain James Lawrence (right foreground) issues his last order— "Don't give up the ship!"—British troops capture the American frigate in 1813. An earlier British attack on the* Chesapeake *had pushed outraged Americans to the brink of war, prompting the British to seek allies among such Indian leaders as Tenskwatawa and Tecumseh.*

Tippecanoe River. After constructing a long council house and a medicine lodge, the brothers and their followers laid out rows of bark *wigewas* (houses) and a huge log cabin, The House of the Stranger, which would shelter the legions of warriors expected to arrive.

The British, meanwhile, were expecting trouble. Anxious about U.S. reaction to their hostile boarding of the *Chesapeake*, they were eager to investigate an alliance with Tenskwatawa, whose anti-American feelings were widely known. Soon after the completion of Prophetstown, British officials invited Tenskwatawa to meet with them in Canada. The invitation was accepted—not by the Prophet Tenskwatawa, but by his warrior brother. Tecumseh was seizing the reins of the Indian resistance movement.

In Canada, Tecumseh let the British know he was not just another chief, but the head of the united Indian movement. Impressed by his regal attitude, the British accepted him on his own terms. Tecumseh reminded them that their broken promises had cost Indian lives at Fallen Timbers. His people, he said firmly, would consider an alliance with the British only if they received major provisions of troops, artillery, and supplies. After meeting him, the British concluded that the Shawnee brothers would be valuable allies if war broke out.

Meanwhile, Tenskwatawa was engaging in his own diplomatic activities. In June, realizing that Harrison was nervous about the rebellious Prophetstown—so near governor's headquarters at Vincennes—Tenskwatawa sent a delegation to see him. The Prophet's representatives told Harrison that their leader wanted "to live in peace with you and your people." He also wanted a

Ojibwa, Sac, and Fox warriors engage in battle on Lake Superior. In 1809, Tecumseh visited these tribes, urging them to form a united front against the land-hungry Americans instead of fighting among themselves.

large quantity of food and tools. Disarmed by Tenskwatawa's benign attitude, Harrison quickly dispatched a shipment of food and farming equipment to Prophetstown. Then he told U.S. officials to stop worrying about Tenskwatawa's movement because he had transformed its leader into a "useful tool" of American policy.

Despite Harrison's supplies, the winter of 1808–9 was a hard one for the people at Prophetstown. They had been too busy building the community to bring in a proper crop, and food was scarce. When cold weather came, some residents survived only by eating their dogs and horses. That winter, the village was also struck by a cholera epidemic; all over the village, people were sick and dying. Worst hit by far were the Ottawas and Chippewas, whose angry survivors blamed Tenskwatawa for the deaths and began returning to their home villages.

But Tecumseh went right on recruiting. In April, he visited the Illinois tribes, meeting with Sacs, Foxes, and Winnebagos. Worried by the construction of a new U.S. fort in their area, these peoples were receptive to the Shawnee leader's message. They gave him not only a warm welcome but the promise of many new warriors for the movement.

Meanwhile, pilgrims continued to flock to Prophetstown. Tenskwatawa had begun preaching less about spiritual matters and more about Indian political and military union, a theme that Harrison regarded with displeasure. Not much earlier, he had considered Tenskwatawa a good influence, believing that his lectures against alcohol and for peaceful behavior would, indeed, lead to peace. He no longer believed that; when he next reported to Washington, he called Tenskwatawa "a liar and a scoundrel."

Nevertheless, Harrison's spies had reported that large numbers of Chippewas and Ottawas had left

Prophetstown because they no longer trusted Tenskwatawa. Concluding that there was now little danger of an Indian uprising—and aware that Tecumseh was out of the area, recruiting warriors for his movement—Harrison decided to push through yet another land purchase from the Northwest tribes.

The resulting Fort Wayne Treaty of 1809—which provided that 3 million acres of Indian land be exchanged for $7,000 and a small annual payment—triggered a blast of rage in Prophetstown. Adding to Tecumseh's fury was his sense of being caught off guard, deluded by wishful thinking. He must have believed that most Indians were so strongly opposed to further land sales that they would stop their chiefs from signing any new treaties. Now he saw he had been mistaken, and his anger was unbounded. Vowing to kill the government chiefs for giving up land that belonged to all Indians, he declared that he and his allies would forcibly turn back any settlers who tried to move onto that land.

In one sense, the Fort Wayne Treaty helped the Indian resistance movement: it showed Indians that Tecumseh had been right all along, that whites had no intention of honoring the Greenville Treaty or any other treaty, and that they would not stop demanding Indian land until they had it all. The treaty also seemed to jolt the Indians out of their complacency, strengthening the Shawnee brothers and diminishing the government chiefs who had gone to Fort Wayne.

In June, Harrison's principal agent and spy, François Dubois, told his chief about a newly militant mood at Prophetstown. Tenskwatawa, the agent told the governor, had begun to speak bitterly about the treachery of whites—Harrison in particular. He had been telling his followers that they had been cheated out of their land, which belonged to all Indians and could not be legally

Holy men perform the medicine dance in a Winnebago longhouse near Lake Michigan. Deeply concerned about the recent erection of an American fort close to their villages, the Winnebagos provided a large number of recruits for Tecumseh's Indian unity movement.

sold by individual leaders. The time was approaching, the Prophet had been saying, for Indians to reclaim what was theirs, by force if necessary.

Making Dubois's report even more unsettling were the rumors about Tecumseh. He had expanded his influence, said the agent, enlisting the support of the Foxes, the Sacs, and other tribes in the West and distant Northwest. People in Prophetstown, Dubois continued, were boasting that Tecumseh now had the strength to raise a 10,000-man army in a week's time and double that number in a month. All these warriors, it seemed, were just waiting for a sign from Tecumseh. When it came, they would pick up their weapons and march on the whites.

Tecumseh's burgeoning strength disturbed even the tough-minded Harrison; he knew he would have to stop the Shawnee chief before things went much further. Both Shawnee brothers, in fact, now occupied a central place in the governor's mind. Deciding first to try being reasonable, he sent a messenge to Tenskwatawa, inviting him to come to Vincennes for a meeting. Now, as he had before, Tecumseh stepped forward: he himself would meet this famous deal-making governor. The conference was set for August 1810 at the governor's residence in Vincennes.

Identifying himself to Harrison as "the head" of the united Indians, Tecumseh asserted that all Indian land was the common property of all Indians and that no single tribal leader could rightfully sell any of it without the consent of the rest. The governor, of course, believed otherwise. He and this war chief were miles apart in background, training, and goals. Living when they did, where they did, they had to be opponents. Still, Harrison could not withhold his admiration for his courageous enemy. Later, writing to colleagues in Washington, D.C., he said:

Tecumseh holds his second meeting with Governor Harrison in Vincennes. "You see him today on the Wabash, and in a short time hear of him on the shores of Lake Erie or Michigan," the governor later said of his adversary, "and wherever he goes he makes an impression favorable to his purpose." Despite his admiration for Tecumseh, Harrison sincerely hoped the Shawnee warrior's crusade would fail.

The implicit obedience and respect which the followers of Tecumseh pay him is really astonishing . . . [It] bespeaks him as one of those uncommon geniuses which spring up occasionally to produce revolutions and overturn the established order of things. If it were not for the vicinity of the United States, he would perhaps be the founder of an Empire that would rival in glory Mexico or Peru.

A year passed before Tecumseh and Harrison met again at Vincennes, but time had altered nothing. Tecumseh still insisted that the land involved in the Fort Wayne Treaty belonged to the Indians and must not be settled by whites. Harrison responded to this view bluntly: "I will put petticoats on my soldiers," he snapped, "sooner than give up a country I have bought fairly from its true owners!"

Although they remained in opposite corners, Tecumseh and Harrison managed to end their conference courteously. Tecumseh said he would soon travel south in order to bring the Indians there into the resistance movement. Meanwhile, he hoped Harrison would permit no settlers to move onto the disputed land. After his southern trip, Tecumseh promised, he would visit Washington, D.C., and "settle all difficulties" with the president.

Reporting on the meeting, Harrison described Tecumseh's whirlwind activities to the U.S. secretary of war: "You see him today on the Wabash, and in a short time hear of him on the shores of Lake Erie or Michigan, or on the banks of the Mississippi; and wherever he goes he makes an impression favorable to his purpose. He is now upon the last round to put a finishing stroke to his work."

But much as he admired Tecumseh, Harrison had to wish that he failed. "I hope," he wrote at the close of his letter to the war secretary, "before [Tecumseh's] return, that that part of the work which he considered complete will be demolished, and even its foundation rooted up."

7

FIGHTING FOR AN INDIAN NATION

Ignoring his aides' pleas to stop, William Henry Harrison spurs his horse into action at the Battle of Tippecanoe. Tecumseh had desperately hoped to avoid open conflict between the military and the residents of Prophetstown, but in the fall of 1811, thanks to the madly egocentric Tenskwatawa, it took place anyway.

After his second meeting with Harrison, Tecumseh headed south with some two dozen of his best warriors. He knew that if he managed to unite the southern tribes with those of the Great Lakes and Ohio Valley regions, he could present a formidable obstacle to further encroachment on Indian lands. He fervently hoped that Harrison would now recognize the strength of the Indians' commitment to their lands—and that, in Tecumseh's absence, he would make no more deals with corrupt chiefs.

Just before he left, Tecumseh told his brother Tenskwatawa to keep preaching, to keep spreading the word about Indian unity, and—most important of all—to keep the peace. Harrison might seize upon his absence to attack, Tecumseh told his brother, and at this stage a war with the whites could destroy the budding unity movement. If the whites moved on Prophetstown, said Tecumseh, Tenskwatawa should lead his people into the woods and stay out of sight until the soldiers left. The Prophet said he understood, and the brothers parted.

Tecumseh expected to reach what he called Mid Day—the completion of a north-south Indian alliance—by early 1812, but he had misjudged the temper of the southern tribes. In the North, 50 years of racial warfare had created deep animosity between Indians and whites; in the South, relations between the tribes and their white neighbors, while not trouble free, were less strained. Because most of the southern Indians were farmers, not hunters, they did not need vast hunting grounds to sustain their pattern of life, as the northern tribes did.

The first stop on Tecumseh's six-month journey was in present-day Alabama, where he met with several important Chickasaw chiefs. As was his custom, he went before them dressed very plainly: he wore a simple breechclout, and his head was clean-shaved except for a thick, braided scalplock hanging down to his shoulders.

The Chickasaws listened respectfully as Tecumseh presented his vision of an Indian confederation, but the idea of banding together with the northern Indians— some of whom had been the Chickasaws' enemies for generations—failed to appeal to them. Politely but firmly, the chiefs refused to join the alliance.

In late September, Tecumseh visited the Choctaw villages in Mississippi. There, he delivered an eloquent and heartfelt speech to several hundred people. "Before the palefaces came among us, we enjoyed the happiness of unbounded freedom," he said. "How is it now? Wants and oppressions are our lot; for are we not controlled in everything? . . . Are we not being stripped day by day of the little that remains of our ancient liberty?"

Tecumseh's listeners stood spellbound. Among those present was Captain Sam Dale, a white soldier and Indian fighter, who later described the Shawnee leader and his speech: "His eyes burned with supernatural lustre, and his whole frame trembled with emotion. His voice resounded over the multitude—now sinking in low and musical whispers, now rising to the highest key, hurling

Pushmataha, chief of the Choctaws, had a long history of cooperation with non-Indians, to whom he had ceded much of present-day Mississippi and Alabama. When Tecumseh tried to recruit men among the Choctaws, Pushmataha called him a "trouble maker" and threatened to execute any warrior who joined him.

out his words like a succession of thunderbolts . . . I have heard many great orators, but I never saw one with the vocal powers of Tecumseh."

But of all the southern tribes, the Choctaws were traditionally the most pro-American. They allowed white Christian missionaries to live among them, and many chose to raise livestock and plant crops in the manner of white farmers. Respected as a strong leader in both peace and war, their chief, Pushmataha, was also known as a splendid orator, said to be the equal of Tecumseh himself. In spite of—or perhaps because of—Tecumseh's extraordinary appeal, Pushmataha responded to his speech with a stinging rebuke.

"I know your history well," Pushmataha told Tecumseh. "You are a disturber. You have ever been a trouble maker. When you have found yourself unable to pick a quarrel with the white man, you have stirred up strife between different tribes of your own race." Pushmataha warned that any Choctaw who tried to join the Shawnee agitator would be put to death. Clearly, Tecumseh's Indian alliance would get little help here.

The orator probably expected a better reception among the Upper Creeks of Alabama; indeed, most of the rank-and-file Creeks responded to Tecumseh and his message with enthusiasm, but their government chiefs, influential men who strongly opposed the resistance movement, deeply distrusted him. Urged by these old leaders to stay away from Tecumseh, most young warriors did. Only 30 joined the cause.

Overall, in fact, Tecumseh's southern swing produced few new allies. Disappointed but not discouraged, he continued to hope that, in time, the southern tribes could be brought around to his way of thinking. And meanwhile, his coalition of northern warriors was growing stronger by the day—or so he thought.

Harrison, who was determined to crush the budding Indian resistance movement before it flowered, had not been idle in Tecumseh's absence. In September 1811, seizing on a minor episode of horse theft as an excuse, he led his 900-man army out of Vincennes and toward the Tippecanoe River village of Prophetstown, 150 miles to the north.

On November 7, the troops made camp on the Tippecanoe, a few miles from Prophetstown. Soon after their arrival, a messenger appeared. Tenskwatawa, whose lookouts had been reporting on the army's movements, sent word that he would meet with Harrison the following day. The message was a ruse: Tenskwatawa had decided—in direct violation of Tecumseh's orders—to attack Harrison's forces. Addressing his people in a burst of mystical speech, the Prophet said the Great Spirit had told him that half the white soldiers were already dead and that the rest had lost their minds. The Indians could easily dispatch them with tomahawks. Any whites who survived and managed to fire would do no harm, because the Prophet's magic had made their bullets useless and the Indians' flesh impenetrable.

Inspired by the Prophet's fiery words and sure of victory, the Prophetstown Indians crept up on Harrison's camp during the night. But Tenskwatawa was no military man; he had sent them too late. Dawn was approaching quickly, and the soldiers were waking up. The element of surprise had been lost. A sentry's shot put the whole camp on alert, and within moments soldiers and Indians were engaged in bloody hand-to-hand combat.

Perched on a rock some distance from the battle, Tenskwatawa intoned a wild war chant that kept his men fighting. In his critically acclaimed 1967 book, *The Frontiersmen*, historian Allan W. Eckert writes of the battle: "Never had Indians been known to fight in so exposed a manner or with such complete abandon. Under the influence of the fanaticism Tenskwatawa had roused in them, they actually rushed right into the bayonets of soldiers."

Meanwhile, racing his horse from one side of the battlefield to the other, Harrison rallied his own troops, ignoring the bullets that struck his hat and grazed his scalp. Watching their apparently fearless commander, the outnumbered soldiers fought fiercely, winning the field soon after daybreak. By that time, the Indians realized that Tenskwatawa had vanished from his rock, and they began slipping off to the surrounding forest.

Dead on the battleground were some 40 Indians and 150 soldiers. Although the Indians had suffered fewer casualties, they had retreated; the victory belonged to

Harrison. As sunlight flooded the scene, the army marched to Prophetstown, now deserted, and burned it to the ground.

Completely disillusioned with Tenskwatawa, the former Prophetstown residents straggled back to their villages. They spread the word of the Tippecanoe disaster and advised their tribes that the Prophet was an imposter and a coward and that the resistance movement should be abandoned altogether.

Tecumseh returned soon after the battle of Tippecanoe. Riding home through the bleak, windswept countryside, perhaps he had a premonition as he approached what once was Prophetstown. In any case, what he saw were the cold, charred ruins of the village—and the end of his dream of a united, peaceful Indian nation. "I stood upon

Harrison's forces decimate those of the Prophet at the Battle of Tippecanoe. Although Tenskwatawa had promised his men that the soldiers' bullets would be "soft as rain," those bullets killed 40 Indians and gave the victory to Harrison. The defeat sharply impaired Tecumseh's unity campaign.

the ashes of my own home," he said later, "and there I summoned the spirits of the warriors who had fallen. And as I snuffed up the smell of their blood from the ground, I swore once more eternal hatred—the hatred of an avenger!"

A handful of Tippecanoe veterans had made a camp near the burned village. There, they awaited Tecumseh's return. Also waiting was Tenskwatawa, whom the loyalists had captured, imprisoned, and condemned to death as a traitor. Before the sentence could be carried out, Tecumseh arrived, fresh from the awful sight of Prophetstown and the news of Tippecanoe.

At the sight of their leader, the Indians shouted with joy, but their voices died as he silently approached the bound figure of Tenskwatawa. After staring at him for several minutes, Tecumseh placed his hunting knife on the prisoner's throat. Then, saying that killing was too honorable a fate, he cut Tenskwatawa's bonds, grabbed his head, shook it savagely, and dropped him.

Mad for glory and power of his own, Tenskwatawa had destroyed the movement his brother had spent 10 years building. Now Tecumseh had no brother. He walked away from the moaning figure at his feet and never looked back. Tenskwatawa would spend his remaining 22 years moving from one village to another, a dishonored and homeless man.

In the spring of 1812, Tecumseh set out for British Canada. He had never wanted to ally the Indian cause with that of the British, but all chances of Indian unity now seemed gone. An alliance with England offered the only hope of driving the Americans off Indian land. British officials indicated strong interest in Tecumseh's plans for the future.

The Shawnee warrior realized that Harrison had learned of his sudden friendship with the British. To placate him until he could reorganize his forces, Tecumseh visited the governor, hinting that he would soon make his promised visit to the president. For the moment, Harrison took him at his word. "I do believe," he noted in a report to Washington, "that the Indians are sincere in their professions of peace and that we will have no further hostilities." Meanwhile, Tecumseh had begun rounding up his dispersed followers and recruiting new ones. Within months, warriors were streaming back to his camp.

Alarmed by these signs of new life in the Indian resistance, Harrison and other leaders called a council of tribal chiefs. The Americans planned to distribute food, blankets, salt, and other supplies to the Indians, but they first intended to get the chiefs to promise not to cooperate with Tecumseh. Then, to the officials' astonishment, the Shawnee leader himself showed up at the council. Assuring both the Americans and the chiefs that he had no intention of making war, he said his people would resort to arms only in self defense, as they had been forced to do at Tippecanoe.

When Tecumseh finished speaking, a number of chiefs rose and said what the Americans wanted to hear. The Shawnee brothers, they asserted, were rash and belligerent; Tecumseh was a troublemaker who should be prevented from leading young warriors into foolish violence. American officials were gratified. What they did not know was that the hostile words were mere window-dressing, spoken to keep them off guard.

After the conference, a Wyandot chief who had made particularly biting remarks about Tecumseh arranged a secret meeting with him. When they were alone, the Wyandot gave Tecumseh a parcel. Sent by British officials in Canada, it contained a belt made of black wampum (shells), the ancient Indian sign for a declaration of war. The British expected Tecumseh to side with them if war

British soldiers and civilians look over the harbor at Amherstburg, Canada, site of Fort Malden. Tecumseh, who was at Malden when he learned that the War of 1812 had started, made the British fort his headquarters, soon assembling hundreds of warriors there to fight the Americans.

broke out. Tecumseh had already decided he would do just that.

British-American relations, shaky since the close of the American Revolution in 1783, had taken a sharp turn for the worse in recent years. By 1812, another war seemed inevitable. Embroiled in a seemingly endless European conflict with the French emperor Napoléon, the British had been harassing American merchant ships trying to trade with France. Not satisfied with appropriating cargoes, the British were also kidnapping American sailors on the high seas and forcing them to serve in the Royal Navy. Enraged, Easterners had begun clamoring for a U.S. declaration of war against England. That demand was echoed and redoubled in the South and West, areas that had their own reasons for wanting a war with Britain.

Florida had long been a haven for escaped slaves, marauding pirates, and hostile Indians. It was still a Spanish possession, but by 1810, most of its permanent settlers were Americans. Bitterly resentful of Spain's failure to protect them from the Indians, the settlers were demanding Florida's annexation to the United States. Because Spain was Britain's ally in the war against Napoléon, a war with Britain would make Spanish territory fair game for the United States. Florida, too, wanted war.

But the loudest war cries came from the West, whose residents accused the British of arming the Indians and inspiring their endless attacks. Most westerners believed that Tecumseh and his brothers were cat's-paws of the British; they saw the Prophet's attack at Tippecanoe and Tecumseh's demand for revenge as part of a British plot. The westerners' accusations contained more than a hint of truth. Indeed, before Harrison's men torched Prophetstown, they had discovered a considerable supply of British weapons.

The British believed that if the Indians did not fight for them, they would fight against them. Writing to the British governor of Canada in 1807, a local official asked, "Are the Indians to be employed in case of a rupture with the United States?" The governor replied, "If we do not employ them, there cannot exist a moment's doubt that they will be employed against us." American fears of a British-Indian alliance were thus firmly grounded in reality.

Harrison and other frontier residents believed that the only way to make the West safe for Americans was to drive the British out of Canada and annex it to the United States. "On to Canada!" became the battle cry of the so-called War Hawks, a group of determined and bellicose young congressmen representing the West. Clearly, the stage was set for war, and in 1812, it came. At the request of President James Madison, Congress declared war on Great Britain on June 18.

That day found Tecumseh on his way to Canada for a meeting with British officials; he learned about the declaration when he arrived. By early July, he had assembled a group of dedicated warriors—Wyandots, Chippewas, Sioux, Shawnees, and other Indians who had never doubted his great powers. Tecumseh rallied his followers at Fort Malden in Amherstburg, Canada, across the river from the U.S. fort in Detroit.

Commanding the newly named Northwestern Army of the United States was the aging Michigan Territory governor William Hull, an officer who had performed nobly in the American Revolution but who had grown fat and indecisive. One month after the declaration of war, Brigadier General Hull left his Detroit headquarters and marched toward Canada with 2,200 men.

Hull started out nervous; his spies had reported the presence of a large concentration of "savages" nearby. Leading these Indians, said Hull's informers, was none other than the legendary war chief Tecumseh. As if that was not bad enough, continued the spies, Tecumseh stayed in close contact with another nemesis: Major General Isaac Brock, commander of the British forces in Canada—and supplier of guns to Tecumseh.

Hull thus began his invasion of Canada in less than high spirits. They sank lower when messengers arrived with the news that Fort Mackinac, a small but strategic American base near Lake Michigan, had fallen to a British-Indian force in mid-July. The victory had been swift, in part because Hull had neglected to tell Mackinac's commandant that a war had started.

Tecumseh, whose own spies had given him ample warning of Hull's approach, had stationed his men along the army's route north. As the soldiers filed through swamp and forest, Indians—unseen and uncounted—peppered them with shots and arrows. Hull, who needed no further evidence that his mission was ill-timed, hastily reversed his march and led his men back to the fort at Detroit, where he believed he would be safe.

When Tecumseh's warriors saw the large American army on its way to Canada, they grew uneasy. Clearly, the United States was capable of mobilizing forces vastly outnumbering those of the British and Indians combined. The Indians began to question the wisdom of joining the British in the war, and many decided to desert their allies and declare neutrality.

As Hull was heading back across the Detroit River, a group of the Indian doubters considered joining him, and they invited Tecumseh to meet with them and discuss changing their allegiance. The Shawnee leader left no doubt about his position. "No!" he thundered. "I have taken sides with the king, my father [an Indian title of respect], and I will suffer my bones to lay and bleach upon this shore before I will recross that stream to join in any council of neutrality."

Tecumseh's eloquent words kept the Indian forces from disintegrating. Adding to their morale was belated news of the fall of Mackinac; that victory also convinced other local Indians that joining with the British was a sound proposition after all. Streams of warriors, including many who had earlier deserted Tecumseh, hastened to Canada to join him.

By now, Tecumseh and his warriors were working closely with General Brock, and the British-Indian campaign had begun to gain momentum. In early August, Tecumseh's men captured an American messenger carrying important information: General Hull had sent Major Thomas Van Horne and 150 men to meet a supply convoy

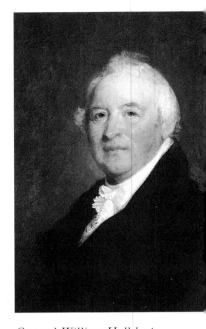

General William Hull had been a noteworthy officer in the American Revolution, but by the time he took command of the U.S. Northwestern Army, his military edge was gone. Nervous and easily confused, he managed to lose Detroit and its 2,200 men to a force half that size led by British general Sir Isaac Brock and Shawnee warrior Tecumseh.

headed for Detroit. Tecumseh wasted no time. With 24 warriors and 40 soldiers, he set out to intercept the American force.

Van Horne never met the convoy; he met Tecumseh. In the war's first non-naval action, the Shawnee's tiny force ambushed and routed the American's larger detachment, whose confused members believed they had been attacked by hundreds of warriors. Van Horne's casualties: 20 dead and 17 wounded; Tecumseh's: 1 dead and 1 wounded—Tecumseh himself, who suffered a painful but nonlethal bullet wound in the thigh.

Tecumseh returned to Fort Malden in glory. Brock was so impressed with the victory—and the victor—that he commissioned him a brigadier general on the spot. Undoubtedly sincere, Brock's tribute was also good strategy. When they learned of Tecumseh's new rank, 700 warriors left their tribes to join him at Fort Malden.

Tecumseh's expanding forces and his defeat of Van Horne made Hull more nervous than ever. Clearly, the security of all the forts under his command was now threatened, and firm action was necessary. After pondering the matter at some length, Hull finally sent a runner to Fort Dearborn in the village of Chicago, ordering its commander to evacuate immediately. Characteristically, however, he had moved too slowly; Tecumseh had already dispatched a large contingent of warriors to the area. Hull's envoy arrived just before the Indians overran the fort and village and slaughtered their defenders.

At this point, Brock wanted to attack Detroit. His officers strongly advised against it, but not Tecumseh. He counseled Brock to move at once, and Brock listened to him rather than to his own officers. On August 14, the general addressed the 1,000 Indians at Fort Malden, proposing the Detroit attack and promising to lead the warriors to a final victory over the Long Knives. Impressed by the general's tough, breezily self-confident

General Sir Isaac Brock, commander of the British forces in Canada, fought alongside Tecumseh for only four months, but the two men formed a deep friendship. Brock called Tecumseh the most "gallant warrior" he had ever known, and of Brock, Tecumseh said simply, "This is a man!"

manner, the Indians answered his speech with ringing cheers. Then Tecumseh turned to his companions and paid Brock the ultimate compliment. "Hooo-eee," he said, "*this* is a man!"

Unlike many generals of the day, the massive, six-foot-three-inch-tall Isaac Brock was not a politician but a dedicated professional soldier, skilled in strategy and given to bold, decisive action—characteristics he shared with Tecumseh. In a report to his superiors in London, Brock said of the Shawnee: "A more sagacious or more gallant warrior does not, I believe, exist."

When Tecumseh outlined his plan for a unified Indian nation in the Old Northwest, Brock supported it enthusiastically and said so in his reports to London. Although Tecumseh responded in the flowery language expected of the era's diplomats, he was genuinely moved. "We, your Indian allies," he said, "are overjoyed that our father beyond the great salt lake [the Atlantic Ocean], the king, has at length awoke from his long sleep and permitted his warriors to come to the assistance of his red children."

By the afternoon of August 15, the two leaders—Brock with 730 men, Tecumseh with 600—had emplaced themselves directly across the river from Detroit. Brock began shelling the fort and sent a message demanding its surrender. The Americans refused. That night, Tecumseh crossed the Detroit River and engineered a classic ruse: he marched his 600 warriors three times in rapid succession across a clearing in front of the fort. The Indians were soon joined by Brock, who was so impressed with Tecumseh's remarkable grasp of military tactics that he removed his wide red sash and gave it to the Shawnee leader as a token of respect and affection.

Hull fell for the ruse. Believing he was threatened by thousands of savages and God knew how many British soldiers, he surrendered the fort and its 2,200 men—the entire Northwestern Army—without a shot. (Two years later, a court-martial sentenced the 61-year-old Hull to death for cowardice and neglect of duty, but because of his age and fine record in the Revolution, he was pardoned by President Madison.)

At noon on August 16, 1812, Brock and Tecumseh rode side by side into the fort to take formal possession. It was a great day for the Indians of the Old Northwest: not even the legendary Pontiac and his rebels had been able to capture Detroit.

8

"WE WISH TO LEAVE OUR BONES UPON THEM"

The fall of Detroit injected new life into the Indian resistance movement. Tecumseh's dream of unity, almost destroyed by Tenskwatawa and his mad quest for personal power, again seemed possible. Indians of many nations, including the Miami, Ottawa, Potawatomi, and Winnebago, flocked to the Shawnee warrior's side.

The Detroit victory, along with those at Fort Dearborn and Chicago, emboldened the Indians to go after even bigger targets: Fort Harrison, an outpost on the Wabash River, and Fort Wayne on the Maumee. If the Indians could knock these garrisons out, Tecumseh reasoned, they could regain control of the Ohio and Indiana territories.

Unfortunately for the Indians, things did not work out that way. Tecumseh had plotted the campaign against the forts with his good friend Brock, but before it started, the British commander was ordered to eastern Canada, which was threatened with an imminent American invasion. Assuring Tecumseh of continued British support in the river-fort campaigns, Brock regretfully departed in early September 1812. He was replaced by Colonel Henry Proctor, a stuffy, old-line officer with absolutely no use for Indians.

Tecumseh had instructed his forces not to attack Fort

Tecumseh inspired many portraits. Not all are entirely accurate; he may, for example, never have worn the swash-buckling outfit illustrated here. The subject's courage, militance, and strength, how-ever, indisputably belong to the great Shawnee warrior.

Harrison or Fort Wayne until he got there with British reinforcements. On September 3, he was still at Fort Malden, trying to persuade the stubborn Colonel Proctor to supply the men and artillery promised by his predecessor. On that day, September 3, the Indians—overconfident after their military successes—struck both Fort Wayne and Fort Harrison. In each case, the American defenders held out through some 10 days of siege, and in each case, the attackers suffered serious losses and then retreated.

Reports of the failed attacks had not yet reached Fort Malden when Proctor finally capitulated to some of Tecumseh's demands. He sent 250 men under the command of Major Adam Muir, along with three cannons, to meet Tecumseh and 800 warriors at the mouth of the Maumee River. On their way to Fort Wayne, the Indian-British army met runners carrying news of the unsuccessful attacks on Fort Wayne and Fort Harrison. That information, along with a series of minor setbacks in transporting the heavy guns, convinced Major Muir to give up the mission and turn back, much to Tecumseh's disgust. Deprived of British firepower, he had no choice but to turn back as well.

Dejected, Tecumseh returned to Fort Malden, where shocking news awaited him: Isaac Brock—at 43, a year younger than his friend Tecumseh—was dead. The gallant officer had been killed in action on October 13, shot while defending the Niagara River peninsula against American invaders. Tecumseh took Brock's death hard. Colonel Proctor took it calmly; he now became a brigadier general and succeeded to Brock's former title, commander in chief of British western military operations. The Indians were stuck with him for the duration of the war.

Tecumseh spent most of the winter of 1812–13 in a state of gloomy reverie. The Detroit and Dearborn victories had promised great things, but the Fort Harrison

Henry Proctor, the British general who replaced Tecumseh's friend Isaac Brock, was as unlike his predecessor as he could be. Stubborn, stuffy, overcautious, and supremely distrustful of Indians, he treated Tecumseh with contempt and, in the end, betrayed him.

and Fort Wayne failures had not. Indian unity seemed further away than ever; friends and relatives were dying in great numbers; Proctor had no real interest in helping the Indians.

As Tecumseh brooded and waited for spring, the Americans were at last waking up to the magnitude of their losses at Detroit and Chicago. If they intended to win this war, they would have to make some changes, starting with the military. Hull had managed to lose most of the original Northwestern Army at Detroit, but in February 1813, the government announced a new and expanded force: the Second Northwestern Army. Named to command it was none other than General William Henry Harrison, by then famous as the hero of Tippecanoe. Tecumseh and his old foe would meet again.

The new commander's first move was to build a large

and sturdy garrison on the Maumee River. Fort Meigs (named for Governor Return J. Meigs of Ohio) would be within striking distance of Fort Malden. Harrison, accompanied by an 1,800-man army, was still directing the construction of Fort Meigs in April, when Tecumseh came back to Fort Malden. By this time, most of the Indians had returned to Malden from their winter grounds. Some 1,500 cheered the arrival of the great Shawnee warrior.

Tecumseh, who had spent February and March recruiting warriors, rode into Malden at the head of 1,000 men. How best to deploy them was the subject of conversation when he met with Proctor, who by now seemed to have changed his attitude toward Indians. Realizing that Tecumseh's warriors could make the difference between success and failure, he spoke to the Shawnee with new respect. Would Tecumseh commit his forces to a joint British-Indian attack on Fort Meigs?

Destruction of the strategically placed garrison, said Proctor, would probably end the Americans' efforts to occupy Michigan and northern Ohio. Indeed, it might end the war with a British-Indian victory. Working hard to gain Tecumseh as an ally, Procter even expressed support for the Shawnee's principal goal in the war: the establishment of an Indian nation that would incorporate all the land north of the Maumee River, including all of Michigan. As an added inducement, Proctor promised that if he and Tecumseh captured William Henry Harrison, Tecumseh could have him to deal with in any manner he chose. Tecumseh said he would join Proctor in assaulting the fort.

The British and Indian forces, some 2,000 strong, left Fort Malden on April 24. A week later, Proctor's artillery and gunboats began shelling Fort Meigs as Tecumseh and his warriors mounted a series of hit-and-run raids. But the Americans, well-protected by the network of trenches they had dug inside the fort's walls, bore the attacks with few casualties.

After several days of indecisive battle, Tecumseh made a surprising move. First consulting with his chiefs, all of whom approved of the plan, he crept up to the wall of the fort and fired an arrow over the top. Wrapped around the arrow's shaft was a message—one that might have been written by an armored knight four centuries earlier:

> To Governor Harrison. We are enemies and we are met here to oppose one another at last. Why should not we, who are the leaders, settle the matter between us alone, so that the blood of our fine young men need not be shed in the fight which presents itself? Meet me in combat on a neutral ground of your choice and with whatever weapon is your choice, or even with none, and I will have the same, or none, and we will then fight this matter out between us until one of us is dead. He who triumphs will then hold this ground and he who has been beaten, his people will immediately return home and remain quiet ever after. My chiefs are in agreement on this head. We are men. Let us meet like men. Let us fight like men. Let us spare our people. I await your answer. Swing a lantern above the gate if you accept. I will be watching and I will then come and meet you for the contest. Tecumseh.

This astonishing document might have changed history—if the white man had agreed to the red man's terms. But he did not. Tecumseh and his followers waited outside the fort's walls for three hours and, when no answer came, returned to their camp. According to reports from inside witnesses, Harrison almost accepted the challenge, then changed his mind. One officer apparently suggested swinging a lantern and then cutting Tecumseh down when he approached. Harrison angrily vetoed this plan.

In early May, 1,200 Kentucky reinforcements arrived at Fort Meigs. Harrison ordered them to slip across the river, disable the enemy's heavy guns, and return immediately. "I take occasion to warn you," he told the men,

"against that rash bravery which is characteristic of the Kentucky troops." After accomplishing their mission, some of the militiamen returned as ordered, but 650 of them did not. Just as Harrison had feared, they recklessly pursued the few dozen Indians who fled the gun emplacements. Watching the Kentuckians from across the river, Harrison was heard to say, "They are lost! They are lost!"

The Americans were behaving just as Tecumseh had hoped they would. He and his men allowed their pursuers to follow them for a mile or two, then abruptly turned and counterattacked. In a few minutes, they killed 100 soldiers and took 500 prisoners; the others escaped to the safety of the fort. Tecumseh took a group of warriors to check the damaged artillery while his lieutenants herded the prisoners into a makeshift stockade.

Later in the day, a messenger brought Tecumseh

After learning that Indians were torturing American prisoners, Tecumseh roars through his own ranks, swinging his tomahawk and shouting at the top of his lungs. So angry was the Shawnee warrior, who had specifically forbidden such abuse, that he killed a disobedient Chippewa outright, shocking the rest of his troops into awed silence.

distressing information: his men were torturing the prisoners. Tecumseh leapt onto his gray mare and galloped to the stockade, where he confronted a grisly sight. Bodies, most of them naked, scalped, and mutilated, lay everywhere. The surviving Americans were huddled in a corner of the stockade from which, one by one, they were being dragged by the Indians.

Tecumseh almost exploded with rage; he had strictly forbidden the abuse of prisoners. Brandishing his war club, he strode up to a knife-wielding Chippewa who was about to slit an American's throat. The tall Shawnee leader commanded the warrior to stop, but he did not: his knife plunged into the prisoner's throat. Not even pausing, Tecumseh raised his club and, with a mighty blow, struck the Chippewa dead. A hush fell over the stockade. The Indians could hardly believe they had seen their leader kill one of them in defense of a white man.

His faced deeply flushed, Tecumseh turned on the warriors and roared, "Did we not direct in council that prisoners at our mercy were not to be tortured or slain?" Then, after saying anyone who wished to kill another American prisoner would have to kill him first, he whirled around to point at Proctor, who had been calmly observing the murders.

"Why have you permitted this?" asked Tecumseh.

"Sir," said Proctor smoothly, "your Indians cannot be commanded."

"Begone!" thundered Tecumseh. "You are unfit to command. Go and put on petticoats!"

Proctor hestitated, then silently left the stockade. Tecumseh placed the surviving Americans under the protection of his own men, then led the rest of his warriors back to battle.

After another few days of indecisive skirmishing, Proctor decided the siege was useless and, over Tecumseh's strenuous objections, ordered the troops to

return to Fort Malden. Appalled by such a halfhearted
method of conducting a war, many Indians quietly
deserted and returned to their homes.

The story of Tecumseh's rescue of the prisoners spread
across the frontier, winning him a large measure of
respect and admiration among the white settlements.
Harrison also heard of the rescue—and of Proctor's earlier
promise to Tecumseh. Addressing a group of chiefs on
the American side, he made his own promise: if they
captured Proctor, they might have him as their personal
prisoner—provided, Harrison said, that "you will treat
him as a squaw and only put petticoats on him, for he
must be a coward who would kill a defenseless prisoner."

In July and August, Tecumseh and Proctor led two
more assaults against the Americans, one of them another
crack at Meigs, the other an attack on Fort Stephenson,
a tiny outpost on the Upper Sandusky River, near Lake
Erie. Humiliatingly, both failed. Harrison's well-supplied,
well-manned stockade stood firm, its soldiers refusing to
emerge for a battle no matter how elaborate a ruse
Tecumseh designed. Fort Stephenson, commanded by a
21-year-old American infantry major and defended by
about 170 men, withstood the assault of a British-Indian
force that outnumbered them by at least 20 to 1.

Overall, American losses had been greater than those
of their enemies, but Harrison's ranks were constantly
swelled by new volunteers, and Proctor's were not. By
mid-1813, the Second Northwestern Army boasted 8,000
troops. With a much smaller population from which to
draw replacement fighters, the British-Indian alliance
faced the growing enemy army with only 2,500 men,
some of them Indians who might desert at any moment.

By now, relations between the British and the Indians
were strained almost to the breaking point. Proctor
disliked the warriors' refusal to conduct by-the-book

sieges; Tecumseh resented Proctor's withholding of military information crucial to the Indians as well as to the British. Proctor was also desperately worried. He was extremely low on food, ammunition, and manpower. Repeated requests to the Canadian governor-general had produced next to nothing.

What worried Proctor most of all was Lake Erie, the shipping route through which Fort Malden received the supplies that made survival possible. British ships still controlled the lake, but Harrison had ordered the construction of a small fleet. Under the command of a young American naval officer, Lieutenant Oliver Hazard Perry, nine new ships materialized on the south side of the lake on August 5. Cruising in sight of Amherstburg and Fort Malden, the American vessels seemed to be taunting the British. As long as they remained, no supplies could reach Proctor and his allies.

R. H. Barclay, commodore of the British fleet on the

Brandishing his sword, 28-year-old Lieutenant Oliver Hazard Perry leaves his damaged flagship for another vessel during the Battle of Lake Erie on September 3, 1813. Perry's trouncing of the British navy terrified General Proctor, who immediately fled Fort Malden, persuading Tecumseh to accompany him.

Detroit River, was very short of hands. But when the governor-general ordered him to "make his appearance on the Lake and meet the enemy," he had little choice. In one of naval history's shortest and most decisive battles, Barclay lost both his entire squadron and control of the vital Lake Erie. Afterwards, Perry sent Harrison a historic message: "We have met the enemy and they are ours." As soon as Perry had repaired his ships, he would transport Harrison and his army across the lake to Fort Malden.

Now seeing himself threatened by both Harrison and Perry, Proctor panicked and ordered Fort Malden evacuated immediately. Typically, he gave Tecumseh no information until the Shawnee leader demanded it. Then he called a council of chiefs and warriors and nervously told them that the British fleet had been lost and that Harrison's invasion of Canada was imminent. That made it necessary, he said, to abandon and burn Fort Malden and to move the army a short distance up the Thames River, where it could stand and fight the American army.

It had never been his intent, Proctor continued, to desert his loyal Indian friends. He had every hope that they would march north with their British allies and fight the Americans at the proper time and place. The Indians in the hall exchanged puzzled, angry glances. They had assumed that they, along with the British, would stand fast at Malden. Had Proctor forgotten that they were fighting this war not to defend Canada but to regain their homeland?

When Proctor finished speaking, the crowded room was absolutely quiet. Then all the chiefs and warriors began to talk at once, many of them speculating on the satisfaction to be gained by killing the double-dealing British general. At last Tecumseh stood, and all voices stopped but his. He began by calmly listing the many lies, half-truths, and broken promises Proctor had given the Indians. Then his tone turned contemptuous.

"You always told us you would never draw your foot off British ground," he said to Proctor, "but now, Father, we see that you are drawing back . . . without seeing the enemy. We must compare our father's conduct to a fat dog that carries its tail on its back but, when affrightened, drops it between its legs and runs off."

The laughter of Indians and soldiers alike interrupted Tecumseh's remarks; everyone seemed to appreciate his insult to the British commander. Even Proctor's secretary, busily taking down everyone's speeches, smiled as he wrote. But when Tecumseh continued, his tone became serious, even pleading:

> Father, *listen!* The Americans have not yet defeated us. . . . We therefore wish to remain here and fight our enemy should they make their appearance. If they beat us, we will then retreat with our father . . . Father, you have got the arms and ammunition which our great father [the British king] sent to his children. If you have an idea of going away, give them to us, and you may go and welcome! For us, our lives are in the hands of the Great Spirit. We are determined to defend our lands and, if it be his will, we wish to leave our bones upon them.

Tecumseh concluded his remarks, and the warriors erupted in a frenzy of wild war cries, hoisting their weapons and shaking them defiantly at the British. Soon, Tecumseh and Proctor sat down for talks. The general told the war chief that the British had lost control of the sea lanes, information he had kept from the Indians.

Harrison, said Proctor, would hit Malden and Amherstburg both by sea and by land, surrounding the undersupplied British-Indian forces and leaving them no means of receiving fresh supplies and ammunition and no escape route. They had their best chance of beating the Americans, he asserted, at a site on the Thames River, about 60 miles east of Detroit and inaccessible to Perry and his fleet. Tecumseh now agreed that it would be necessary to abandon Fort Malden, but he told Proctor he would confer with his chiefs before committing them to the plan.

During the all-night council that followed, Tecumseh said he would keep none of the chiefs bound to their promise to fight. He foresaw defeat and would honor any who chose to return home. About half the chiefs, representing some 1,200 of the remaining 2,500 warriors, accepted Tecumseh's release and said they would lead their troops back to their own villages.

In late September, after torching Fort Malden and the shipyards at Amherstburg, the British and Indian forces began their retreat. A minor skirmish on the way—in which Tecumseh received a flesh wound from an American rifle—convinced many more warriors to abandon the fight. Now only about 500 remained. Camped on the banks of the Thames on October 4, Tecumseh addressed his troops. He expected the final battle to take place the next day, he said in a somber voice, and in that battle, he would die.

Gathered around the campfire, the Indians gasped, then fell silent as Tecumseh removed the feathered headband, bear-claw necklace, and other ornaments that identified him as a chief. He distributed them, along with his pistols, rifle, tomahawk, and the sword that Brock had given him as a token of respect, among his closest friends and lieutenants. He would go into battle armed only with the war club that his brother Chiksika had given him many years before. Heads bowed, the Indians accepted Tecumseh's gifts. No one doubted his words.

The next day, October 5, Tecumseh and his warriors joined Proctor at the battle site the general had selected, a carriage road that ran along the river. Proctor's 600

Tecumseh (left foreground) falls during the Battle of the Thames on October 5, 1813. Seconds later, shouts rang out: "Tecumseh is dead! Retreat! Retreat!" With his death, the long fight ended; along with the gallant Shawnee warrior, the Indian resistance movement became history.

men lined up on either side of the road, their cannon placed between the lines. Tecumseh scattered his warriors in the nearby marsh and forest. Then they waited.

In mid-afternoon, sharp bugle notes announced the arrival of the 3,000 soldiers Harrison had sent in pursuit of the British-Indian forces. The American general concentrated on the British troops first, believing that if he could drive them off, the Indians would flee. This was not Britain's finest hour. Led by Proctor and his officers, the king's troops cut and ran after no more than five minutes of fighting, without firing their cannon even once. They left the Indians to meet Harrison's all-out assault alone.

First, 20 American cavalrymen rode into the Indian camp. The Indians picked off a number of them, but they were followed by wave after wave of horsemen and foot soliders, all of them pouring a deadly hail of bullets into the Indians' midst. American survivors later recalled that through the raging gunfire and smoke, they distinctly heard the voice of Tecumseh, shouting, "Be brave! Be strong!" The veterans also remembered seeing the bare-chested Tecumseh dashing from one tree to another, furiously swinging his war club and downing Americans left and right.

The outcome was inevitable: with six times as many men as the Indians, the Americans won easily. The battle ended when a tall Indian, wearing only buckskin trousers and buffalo-hide moccasins, fell to the ground with a bullet in his heart. The Indians knew at once what had happened. "Tecumseh is dead! Retreat! Retreat!" shouted first one warrior, then another. Following the orders their leader had given them, the warriors left the battlefield and melted into the forest.

The War of 1812 would continue for another 14 months, ending in an American victory. In 1840, 27 years after the battle on the Thames, William Henry Harrison—still nicknamed Tippecanoe and still celebrated as the man who vanquished the mighty Tecumseh—would be elected president of the United States. As for the Indians of the Old Northwest, the war ended on October 5, 1813. The Indian resistance movement died with Tecumseh.

But as long as there are people to tell the story, Tecumseh lives. No bullet, no lost battle, could extinguish the fiery spirit of this extraordinary man—military genius, statesman, revolutionary leader, gallant idealist. Face to face with the tide of history, Tecumseh tried almost singlehandedly to turn it back, to return to his people the birthright they lost to the relentless flow of "civilization." He failed, but he proved that nothing can destroy the will of a human being who seeks justice and is willing to fight for it.

CHRONOLOGY

1768	Born on March 9 near present-day Oldtown, Ohio
1783	Participates in Shawnee attacks on American flatboats on Ohio River; takes stand against abuse of prisoners
1787–90	Takes part in Shawnee raids on settlements in Tennessee and Kentucky; after death of brother Chiksika in 1789, becomes leader of Shawnee war party
1791	Leads Indians into battle against Americans on Wabash River, inflicting the U.S. Army's most one-sided defeat in history
1794	Fights under Chief Blue Jacket in Battle of Fallen Timbers, a decisive defeat of Indians by U.S. general "Mad Anthony" Wayne
1795	Boycotts deliberations on the Treaty of Greenville, in which Indians sign over immense land tracts to Americans
1800–1803	With followers, creates and moves into traditional Shawnee village near present-day Indianapolis; acts as mediator in Indian-settler disputes; inaugurates tribal unity crusade
1804	Younger brother changes name to Tenskwatawa—the Prophet—and starts a popular religious movement among Old Northwest Indians
1808	Tecumseh and his brother settle in a new village, Prophetstown, on the Tippecanoe River
1810	Tecumseh meets with Indiana Territory governor William Henry Harrison to denounce American land acquisition under the Fort Wayne treaty of 1809
1811	Travels through South, seeking new recruits; in his absence, Harrison marches on Prophetstown and defeats Indians led by Tenskwatawa at Battle of Tippecanoe
1812	Tecumseh joins British-Indian force led by British general Isaac Brock; aids in capture of U.S. fort at Detroit in War of 1812
1813	With British general Henry Proctor, lays unsuccessful seige to Harrison's army at Fort Meigs, Ohio; betrayed by Proctor and killed by Harrison's forces at the Battle of the Thames on October 5

FURTHER READING

Eckert, Allan W. *The Frontiersman: A Narrative.* Boston: Little, Brown, 1967.

————. *Sorrow of the Heart: The Life of Tecumseh.* New York: Bantam, 1992.

Edmunds, R. David. *Tecumseh and the Quest for Indian Leadership.* Boston: Little, Brown, 1984.

————. *The Shawnee Prophet.* Lincoln: University of Nebraska Press, 1983.

Nevins, Allan and Henry Steele Commager. *A Short History of the United States.* 6th ed. New York: Knopf, 1984.

O'Neil, Paul. *The Frontiersmen.* Alexandria, VA: Time-Life Books, 1977.

Shorto, Russell. *Tecumseh and the Dream of an American Indian Nation.* Englewood Cliffs, NJ: Silver Burdett Press, 1989.

Sugden, John. *Tecumseh's Last Stand.* Norman: University of Oklahoma Press, 1944.

Tanner, Helen Hornbeck. *Atlas of Great Lakes History.* Norman: University of Oklahoma Press, 1987.

Utley, Robert M. and Wilcomb E. Washburn. *Indian Wars.* Boston: Houghton Mifflin, 1977.

Williams, Harry T., et al. *A History of the United States to 1877.* New York: Knopf, 1969.

INDEX

PICTURE CREDITS

ROBERT CWIKLIK holds a B.A. from George Washington University and lives in New York City. His books for young adults include *Sequoyah and the Cherokee Alphabet*, which was cited by the New York Public Library as one of 1991's Best Books for the Teen Age, and *The Secret History of Grammar*.

W. DAVID BAIRD is the Howard A. White Professor of History at Pepperdine University in Malibu, California. He holds a Ph.D. from the University of Oklahoma and was formerly on the faculty of history at the University of Arkansas, Fayetteville, and Oklahoma State University. He has served as president of both the Western History Association, a professional organization, and Phi Alpha Theta, the international honor society for students of history. Dr. Baird is also the author of *The Quapaw Indians: A History of the Downstream People* and *Peter Pitchlynn: Chief of the Choctaws* and the editor of *A Creek Warrior of the Confederacy: The Autobiography of Chief G. W. Grayson*.